W9-AXZ-349

PRAISE FOR

PARENTING with POSITIVE BEHAVIOR SUPPORT

"Research-based. Respectful. Engaging. Relevant. Practical. Concise. All of these descriptors are my first impressions of *Parenting with Positive Behavior Support*. Some books are 'nice to have' and others are 'need to have.' This is a need to have book for families who have children with problem behavior and for professionals who support those families."

—Ann Turnbull, Ed.D.
Co-director
Beach Center on Disability
The University of Kansas

"This book is a remarkable achievement. It combines the most current perspectives on positive behavior support with a supremely practical format that will be useful for all parents. This book represents a major advance in making the fruits of research accessible for families."

—Glen Dunlap, Ph.D.
Professor
Division of Applied Research and Educational Support
University of South Florida
President of the Association for Positive Behavior Support

"Finally, a book written on positive behavior support specifically for parents. Breaking the cycle of children's difficult behavior is not easy. This book demystifies the process by offering practical guidelines based on solid information and research to help parents think about and approach their children's problem behaviors differently and successfully. Parents will find this book helpful whether designing their own behavior support plan or working collaboratively with professionals to develop plans for home, school, or other settings. Professionals will like this book as well—it's a great resource for planning with families and for generating new ideas about effective supports for children."

—Linda M. Bambara, Ed.D.
Professor
Special Education Department
Lehigh University

"This helpful guide represents the accumulated wisdom of parent/researchers who've been there. The first book written specifically for parents, it will be the positive behavior support 'bible' for all families in need of help with their child's problem behavior."

—V. Mark Durand, Ph.D.
Regional Vice Chancellor
Office of Academic Affairs
University of South Florida St. Petersburg
Author, *Sleep Better!*

"A thoroughly readable, clear, and practical approach to addressing children's problem behavior. Parents, get this book and enrich the life of your family!"

—Edward Carr, Ph.D.
Leading Professor
Department of Psychology
State University of New York at Stony Brook
Co-author, *Communication-Based Intervention for Problem Behavior*
Director
Home-Based PBS for Children with Autism Spectrum Disorder
(funded by New York State Office of Mental Retardation and Developmental Disabilities)

"This guide is a wonderful resource for parents as well as direct care staff who work with children and adolescents who have a history of problem behavior within home and community contexts. The practices promoted by the authors are reflective of state of the art positive behavior support and the guide is written in a manner that makes it easily accessible and very user-friendly."

—Tim Knoster, Ed.D.
Bloomsburg University of Pennsylvania
Department of Exceptionality Programs
Executive Director of the Association for Positive Behavior Support
Co-chair of TASH's Positive Approaches Committee

"[This book] is a practical guide that will help parents design a program of PBS that is a good fit for their child and family. It encourages consistency, involvement of other family members, and it offers hope. It will also serve as an important planning tool when working with professionals about PBS. Hats off! This will be a help in managing difficult behavior and building self-esteem for the child and the parent. I envision parents connecting with other parents to share the good news about what is working well."

—Connie Ginsberg
Executive Director
Family Connection of South Carolina, Inc.
Statewide Parent to Parent Program

PARENTING
WITH POSITIVE
BEHAVIOR
SUPPORT

PARENTING
WITH POSITIVE
BEHAVIOR
SUPPORT

A PRACTICAL GUIDE TO RESOLVING YOUR CHILD'S DIFFICULT BEHAVIOR

by

Meme Hieneman, Ph.D.
University of South Florida St. Petersburg
St. Petersburg, Florida

Karen Childs, M.A.
University of South Florida
Tampa, Florida

and

Jane Sergay, M.Ed.
Comprehensive Family Literacy Services
Tampa, Florida

Baltimore • London • Sydney

Paul H. Brookes Publishing Co.
Post Office Box 10624
Baltimore, Maryland 21285-0624

www.brookespublishing.com

Typeset by Auburn Associates, Inc., Baltimore, Maryland.
Manufactured in the United States of America by
Sheridan Books, Inc., Chelsea, Michigan.

The case studies appearing in this book are composites based on the authors' experiences; these case studies do not represent the lives or experiences of specific individuals, and no implications should be inferred.

Seventh printing, June 2018.

Library of Congress Cataloging-in-Publication Data

Hieneman, Meme.
  Parenting with positive behavior support : a practical guide to
    resolving your child's difficult behavior / by Meme Hieneman, Karen
    Childs, and Jane Sergay.
      p.   cm.
  Includes bibliographical references and index.
  ISBN-13: 978-1-55766-865-3 (pbk.)
  ISBN-10: 1-55766-865-5 (pbk.)
    1. Parenting.   2. Behavior modification.   I. Childs, Karen.
II. Sergay, Jane.   III. Title.
  HQ755.8.H52 2006
  649'.64—dc22   2006018180

British Library Cataloguing in Publication data are available from the British Library.

Contents

About the Authors

This book was written by three women—Meme, Karen, and Jane. Each author is a parent as well as a professional with extensive experience working with children with behavioral difficulties and their families. They have children, although their children are at very different stages in their lives; supportive partners; networks of family and friends; and active community lives. Collectively, Meme, Karen, and Jane have had more than 50 years of professional experience. Within each of their professional roles, they have taken research-based information and applied it in practical ways to improve the lives of children and families.

Meme, Karen, and Jane also have certain shared values that should be evident throughout this book. Although each author has a unique perspective derived from her own personal experiences, all three authors believe in enhancing support and structure in families' lives, being positive and encouraging rather than reactive and punitive, and handling problems in respectful and effective ways.

Meme Hieneman, Ph.D., Director of the Positive Family Intervention Project and Courtesy Assistant Professor in Psychology, College of Arts and Sciences, University of South Florida St. Petersburg, 140 7th Avenue South, St. Petersburg, Florida 33701

Meme Hieneman is a full-time mother and part-time faculty member directing a research project focused on educating parents of children with severe behavior problems at the University of South Florida St. Petersburg. She has two young sons (ages 4 and 6) who are thoughtful, energetic, and generally well behaved but are also typical in that they test her skills and patience on a regular basis. She has a husband who is a true partner in parenting. Following the birth of her first child, Meme decided to leave her full-time employment to stay at home with her children. She now balances a life of volunteering at her children's schools, arranging play dates and extracurricular activities, and engaging in rewarding professional outlets. In her professional career, Meme has worked for more than 20 years with children with severe behavior problems, as well as with their families, educators, and other service providers. While working full-time, Meme was employed as a group home manager, behavior specialist for a school district, staff member for a program assisting families and professionals of children with autism and related disorders, director of a statewide project helping schools to implement positive behavior support (PBS), and co-training coordinator for the Rehabilitation Research and Training Center on Positive Behavior Support.

Karen Childs, M.A., Technical Assistance Specialist for Florida's Positive Behavior Support Project, Department of Child and Family Studies, University of South Florida, 13301 Bruce B. Downs Boulevard, Tampa, Florida 33613

Karen Childs is the mother of two: an 11-year-old daughter emerging into adolescence and a 15-year-old son on the edge of adulthood. In addition to managing her children's school, church, sports, and social activities, Karen focuses her professional career on guiding the development, use, and evaluation of schoolwide PBS systems and helping teachers and families support children with challenging behavior. When Karen has time to herself, she enjoys endurance sports, including triathlons and marathons. Karen's professional experiences include teaching students labeled as severely emotionally disturbed, conducting research on PBS for children with difficult behavior, coordinating state centers on family involvement in education, and training parents and educators on family involvement and the transition into kindergarten. This variety of experiences has proven to be very useful to Karen in dealing with the many kinds of challenges that she faces in her most important role as a parent.

Jane Sergay, M.Ed., Parent Education Specialist and Resource Teacher for the Department of Adult and Community Education, Comprehensive Family Literacy Services, School District of Hillsborough County, 2322 North Tampa Street, Tampa, Florida 33602

Jane Sergay has raised three daughters, now all in their 20s, with her husband Stephen, a neurologist in Tampa: Amanda, a physician; Rebecca, a law student; and Samantha, a college sophomore. Now that her children are grown, her time to reflect has deepened her insight and broadened her perspectives on the importance of the quality of parenting and the extent of challenges families face as they try to parent effectively and well. Jane developed a parent education program when her children were young and continues to teach positive parenting skills to groups and individuals. She has continuously focused her work on enhancing the well-being of children and their families. Jane was involved in researching qualities of effective parenting and guiding parents in teaching basic skills to their children with exceptional needs at the Harvard Graduate School of Education. She taught classes in child development at Lesley College and directed programs that emphasize parent involvement in the schools at the University of South Florida. Her dedications to raising children and supporting the efforts of others have been central themes for her and continue to be the most treasured and significant accomplishments of her life.

Note to the Reader

This book is written especially for you, the parent or caregiver of a child with behavior you would like to see improve. By reading *Parenting with Positive Behavior Support: A Practical Guide to Resolving Your Child's Difficult Behavior* and applying its concepts to the examples in the book and your real life, you will learn to use an effective problem-solving process called positive behavior support (PBS) to resolve your child's difficult behavior and improve your family life in general. Prior to launching into the content of the book, we thought it would be beneficial to share our reasons for writing the book and explain the book's uses and special features.

OUR REASONS FOR WRITING THE BOOK

For as long as we have been parents and involved in professional careers utilizing PBS, writing a book on PBS specifically for parents has been a goal of ours. The reasons we felt this was important were that 1) we knew first hand the benefits PBS could offer families and 2) there were no comprehensive, user-friendly materials for parents and/or nonprofessional caregivers on this topic.

Over the years, we have found that even with our experience and professional training, parenting can be extremely difficult. At times, each of us has been challenged, frustrated, and exhausted by our children's seemingly normal behavior. Through our professional experiences, we knew how effective PBS could be for structuring settings and resolving behavior problems. As a result of the challenges we faced as parents and our backgrounds in PBS, we have each made efforts to integrate PBS into our own child-rearing practices—and experienced the positive results. Employing the principles of PBS with our children and families has allowed us to be more proactive, creative, and loving with our children and to address behavior problems more effectively and efficiently.

Although PBS has been consistently demonstrated to be effective with children and in schools, few materials have been developed for parents on this topic and, of those available, none were written in a way that would allow most parents to easily absorb the materials and put the approach into action. Whereas many books and training programs on parenting and discipline are available to the general public through the mass media, none of these materials have fully described the principles or processes of PBS. These public-oriented materials offer good ideas and strategies, but they do not provide an integrated framework for teaching parents to solve their own behavior problems and to choose appropriate behavioral intervention options for their children and families. Through *Parenting with Positive Behavior Support*, we were able to combine our professional and personal experiences to create a user-friendly workbook on PBS specifically for parents.

FOR WHOM THE BOOK IS INTENDED

This book is intended for parents of children experiencing typical problems with behavior and possibly more significant difficulties. It also may be beneficial for other caregivers who are involved regularly in the lives of the children or families, including people such as teachers, baby sitters, grandparents, coaches, and therapists.

In addition to parents and caregivers, parent educators and other professionals working with families may find this book to be a practical resource. The book's organization, examples, and activities are well suited for training seminars and other instructional formats.

AN EXPLANATION OF THE WRITING STYLE

There are certain special features in how this book is written. First, given that this book was written for parents and by parents, we wanted it to speak directly to you. Given that we are parents ourselves, faced with many of the same issues and challenges you experience, we chose to write the book from a collective *we* voice. When we say *we* throughout the book, we mean both you and us and also all other people involved in the life of your child and family.

Second, we have made every effort to avoid unnecessary jargon. Although we have tried to be as precise as possible, in many cases we have substituted lay terms or even slang to get our point across.

Third, we avoid being directive (e.g., saying, "You should") and instead give options or present considerations to guide your personal decision making. PBS is not a set of methods but rather an individualized, problem-solving process where the strategies are chosen by you based on your own needs and circumstances.

HOW TO GET THE MOST FROM THE BOOK

Parenting with Positive Behavior Support is intended to be a practical guide for parents to use when faced with their children's behavioral challenges. It also creates a framework that parents can use to maximize positive interactions among all family members. To get the most benefit out of this resource, we recommend that you do the following:

Apply what you learn: Read for understanding, thinking deeply about how the principles, framework, and process of PBS relate to your child and family and applying what you learn through the case examples and exercises. The ultimate value of PBS is being able to internalize its principles and process.

Be creative about strategies: Avoid limiting yourself to the ideas presented within this book; they may or may not work for your child and family. PBS is a problem-solving process, not a cookbook of intervention options. You should generate solutions based on your unique circumstances, resources, and needs.

Work with other people: Make every effort to engage the people who know your child and family best, who interact with you on a regular basis, and who may influence the outcome of your effort to change behavior. The people in your life have the ability to either reinforce or interfere with the PBS process.

Integrate other approaches: If appropriate and necessary, combine PBS with other ideas, approaches, or services (e.g., counseling, medical interventions) that may benefit your child or family. PBS is not intended to be exclusive of other methods that may help your child and family.

Thank you for picking up this book. We hope PBS is as helpful for you as it has been for us.

Acknowledgments

This book is the result of our efforts to integrate, repackage, and apply positive behavior support for use by families. The general principles and practices we describe are not of our creation but are the contributions of a great number of researchers and practitioners, many of whom are represented in the Bibliography. We deeply value their work and sincerely hope that we have done their ideas justice.

In particular, we want to acknowledge our mentor and friend, Glen Dunlap, for his support and guidance with this project. We also appreciate the ideas and assistance of other people who provided feedback on earlier drafts, including

Don Kincaid

Brad Hieneman

Tim Knoster

Peggy Quarantello

Susan Moorhead

Delores Razman

We are thankful for the assistance of Rebecca Lazo and the rest of the competent and encouraging staff at Paul H. Brookes Publishing Co. who kept our vision alive while designing and producing this book.

And finally, we would like to thank our families and friends for their patience and encouragement throughout this process. Without them we would not have been able to complete this book.

This book is dedicated to all parents who have responded to their baby's cries even when they thought they were too tired to move; waited patiently so that their child could tie his or her shoe laces even though they knew they would be late; stayed up late at night doing laundry, packing lunches, or making other preparations to help each day go smoothly; remained calm and resolute in imposing a restriction even when their child argued, pleaded, and cried; and waved goodbye as their child left their home for a trip, for college, or forever—hoping that they had imparted the skills, knowledge, and values their child needed to be safe, happy, and productive in the real world.

We know that—just like us—you endeavor to be the best possible parent and struggle with difficult decisions regarding how to raise your children and address their behavior. We hope that this book will provide some additional insights or guidance as you continue on this wonderful journey.

Introduction and Overview

The Basics of Positive Behavior Support

Raising children may be the most important and challenging job we will ever have. This statement has been made many times and may sound cliché, but it is true that we are charged with shaping our children into responsible, caring, and productive adults—a seemingly overwhelming task. Over the years, we worry about our children developing healthy habits, having positive relationships, and learning the skills they will need to be successful. At times, we may feel confident in our ability to guide and support our children, while also juggling everything else we need to do. At other times, we may feel confused or frustrated in our role as parents.

One thing that is likely to challenge us the most is our children's behavior. We become exasperated when our children do not do what they are told, say mean or inappropriate things, or hurt other people. In response, we may try various tactics to get our children's behavior under control—sometimes with successful results, sometimes with detrimental effects, and sometimes without any change at all. While engaged in this search for solutions, we may be concerned that the way our children are behaving and the way we are responding to those behaviors will establish patterns that will last a lifetime. Given all of this, we seek a consistent and effective approach to encouraging positive behavior and dealing with problems that will help our children to become happy, fulfilled, and competent adults.

Parenting with Positive Behavior Support: A Practical Guide to Resolving Your Child's Difficult Behavior describes an approach called positive behavior support (PBS) that has been demonstrated to be effective in schools and community programs and can be extremely helpful in family settings. PBS helps us change how we structure our homes and lives and alter the ways in which we respond to our children so that we can deal more confidently and effectively with our children's behavior. This approach involves a problem-solving process that helps us understand why our children behave the way they do and develop solutions to encourage the behaviors we want and prevent or discourage the behaviors that we do not want.

The value of PBS in addressing difficult behavior has been repeatedly demonstrated in research and real life (including with the children and families of the authors of this book). The principles and practices, although initially designed for people with the most severe disabilities and problem behavior, are now used effectively with a broader range of people and situations. Children with severe and long-standing problem behaviors such as tantrums, defiance, and aggression have experienced life-changing results, including a significant reduction or even elimination of these behaviors (see the Bibliography at the end of the book for citations on research). In addition, PBS has had a broader impact in the lives of children and families, allowing them to participate in more activities, frequent new places, spend more time with people, and simply function more effectively. The degree to which PBS fits and offers benefits for families will become apparent throughout this book.

Parenting with Positive Behavior Support is divided into four sections. Section I provides an overview and introduction to PBS and its role in raising and supporting children in their everyday lives. Section II offers a step-by-step process for addressing problems. Section III shares stories of the PBS process for three specific children. Section IV discusses how parents can integrate PBS into their lives and families and overcome barriers to successfully implement PBS. Each section includes a variety of examples and practice activities to reinforce the information provided.

Section I is divided into two chapters. Chapter 1 focuses on what types of behavior can present a problem, why it is necessary to address problem behavior, and how problem behavior might be addressed. Chapter 2 provides an overview of PBS, including its underlying assumptions and features, as well as why PBS is important for parents and others involved in raising children.

CHAPTER 1

Understanding and Addressing Behavior

Your 2-year-old whines, clings to your leg, and repeatedly asks to be picked up, making it nearly impossible to make dinner, talk on the telephone, or even read your mail.

Your 9-year-old yells, refuses to share his things, and calls his sister names until she cries. If she tries to fight back, he becomes physically aggressive. Even spanking does not seem to make a difference.

Your 14-year-old is extremely limited in the topics she is willing to discuss and activities in which she will participate. You feel that this is interfering with her ability to make friends and become more independent.

As parents, what should we do to address such problems? When our children behave in ways that concern us, we are faced with difficult decisions regarding which behaviors are acceptable and not acceptable, whether it makes sense to intervene, and how we could go about addressing the behavior. These decisions are value judgments and require us to think carefully about our beliefs and the unique characteristics, needs, and priorities of our children and families. This chapter explores these issues, including what constitutes problem behavior and when, how, and why we choose to intervene.

WHAT CONSTITUTES PROBLEM BEHAVIOR?

Because this book is about how to deal with behavior in positive and effective ways, it is necessary to first explain what behavior is and what types of behavior may constitute a problem. The term *behavior* refers to everything that people say or do. It includes talking, walking, touching, and moving. Behavior, in itself, is not a problem. It is simply how people negotiate their way through life. Yet, there are some behaviors that people typically consider problematic, such as having temper tantrums (e.g., screaming, throwing things), hurting other people, talking back or arguing with people in authority, or refusing to comply with directions.

Behaviors come to be seen as problematic because of the effects they have on the children engaging in the behavior, other people, or the surroundings—or because the behaviors simply do not fit within routines or homes. Table 1 lists what we call "the Big Ds"—some categories of behavior that people often associate with problem behavior.

Table 1. The Big Ds

Dangerous: The behavior could hurt the child or someone else.

Example: Jasmine bites other children when she is angry.

Destructive: The behavior may result in destruction of property.

Example: Miguel bends and breaks his father's computer disks.

Disruptive: The behavior upsets or interferes with the overall harmony of the home or other places (e.g., restaurant, park).

Example: Alissa argues loudly when she is told no.

Disgusting: The behavior leads to disapproval or avoidance.

Example: David picks his nose and eats the boogers or wipes them on things.

Developmentally inappropriate: The behavior is typical of a younger child, but not considered normal for a child at that age.

Example: Tyrone cries several times each day. (If he were 6 months old, crying would be normal—it is an infant's primary way of communicating needs. If Tyrone is 8 years old, however, he should have other, more age-appropriate ways to express his needs.)

Whether we see behavior as a problem in need of intervention depends on a number of things. One is how serious the behavior is. Dangerous or destructive behaviors usually require us to act immediately to make sure that our families, friends, and surroundings stay safe. Other (disruptive, disgusting, or developmentally inappropriate) behaviors may be irritating or disturbing but are not really damaging. We decide to address these behaviors when they become especially bothersome or interfere with our children's or families' success and happiness.

Another consideration is whether a problem behavior happens just once or twice or has become a long-standing pattern. *Patterns* are ongoing behaviors or ingrained reactions to circumstances. They can become unproductive and entrenched and have a negative impact on the lives of our children and families. Whereas individual incidents of what we consider "bad behavior" are perfectly normal (for everyone, not just children), problem behaviors that happen frequently or for extended periods of time usually signal that the behavior needs to be addressed.

Individual and family values form a final and very important consideration in deciding if a particular behavior is a problem. Everyone is different, and these differences affect whether we perceive certain behaviors as problems (as well as what kinds of responses we see as acceptable). Our ideas about the acceptability of behavior may have been shaped by a variety of things, including what our parents expected of us as children and our personal experiences with behavior and formal education (e.g., participation in teacher preparation or management training). These ideas may also be influenced by what is considered to be acceptable in our culture and community, among a host of other factors.

In summary, what constitutes a problem should be determined based on our individual values and circumstances and the degree to which the behavior affects our children, families, and communities. Prior to making a decision to intervene with our children's behavior, we should think carefully about our preferences and priorities—choosing our battles based on the issues described in this section.

☀ Activity: Prioritizing Behaviors

List each of your child's behaviors of concern, ranking them from 1 to 5 (in order of greatest to least concern). Decide if each behavior is worthy of addressing and cross off those that are not. Consider the Big Ds and the other criteria described in this section in making your decisions.

1. _____

2. _____

3. _____

4. _____

5. _____

CONSIDERATIONS FOR ADDRESSING BEHAVIOR

As mentioned previously, periodic problems with behavior may be just a typical part of growing up (e.g., "terrible twos," adolescent rebellion). When problem behaviors are allowed to continue over a period of time, get more serious, and then become longstanding patterns, however, they can have lasting effects on our children, our families, and other people in our lives. In this case, we have not only the right, but also the responsibility to intervene.

Impact of Behavior Problems

Problem behavior can impact our children and families in a variety of ways. Some of the effects of problem behavior (and therefore reasons why we might choose to address our children's behavior) are described in this section.

Delay of Learning and Development

The time children spend engaged in problem behavior may actually detract from their involvement in other, more positive activities. Children with behavior problems may be less cooperative in situations in which they could be learning new skills. For example, they might have trouble sitting still to read, participating in team sports, or playing nicely with kids their age. Because they are so disruptive or resistant, they may miss out on important experiences. As a result, problem behavior may stunt our children's social, intellectual, and even physical growth.

Disruption of Family and Community Life

Problem behavior does not just bother the person engaging in the behavior; it can affect everyone around that person. Children's behavior problems can create stress in marriages, disrupt family routines, and interfere with overall family harmony. Problem behavior can also have a domino effect; one family member acts out and pretty soon the whole house is in an uproar. Ultimately, family members and other people caring for children with behavior problems may find that they have given up potentially valuable experiences, such as eating dinner or playing games together, because of the chaos that ensues.

Alienation of Children and Families

Sometimes families of children with problem behavior come to feel isolated from their community because the parents or caregivers worry about how other people will react to their children's misbehavior. They may find it hard to go places such as restaurants, stores, and community events. Parents may find that they are turning down invitations, avoiding outings, and limiting the people with whom they interact because they are anticipating problems. If it is particularly bad, problem behavior can result in children being suspended from school or asked to leave child care centers, public establishments, or events.

Damage to Relationships

Having to deal with problem behavior on an ongoing basis can damage parents' relationships with their children and other family members. It is often exhausting and emotionally draining, particularly if parents believe that they are doling out discipline (especially punishment) constantly—rather than spending that valuable time snuggling, playing with, or simply enjoying their children. Parents may come to view and approach their children negatively. They might find themselves arguing with their spouses over "what to do with that kid" or making accommodations that are unfair to other family members. This can cause parents to feel detached from their children and families.

Relationship problems can also occur outside the home. Children with behavior problems may have difficulty making and keeping friends, as well as interacting with other adults. As a result, they may be left out of important childhood activities such as birthday parties, sleepovers, or hanging out in the neighborhood.

These are some but certainly not all of the reasons why addressing problem behavior may be important for children and families. Failure to intervene effectively and change these patterns may mean that little problems become big problems that have long-term negative outcomes.

Intervention Considerations

Evaluating the acceptability of our children's behavior and determining whether to intervene is difficult. We must recognize that deliberately trying to change another person's behavior can be intrusive. Whereas it is certainly our role as parents to guide and shape our children's behavior, we must weigh our concerns and plans for influencing their behavior against any potential cost to our children, families, or ourselves.

We might consider the impact of intervention on our parent–child relationships and our children's self-confidence. It may be a good idea to ask questions such as, "Will my child see me as a tyrant?" or "Will my child feel that he or she is losing control?" We also might want to consider the timing. For example, it may be worth asking, "Does it make sense to address this behavior now, while my child is getting used to a new school?" Finally, we might want to evaluate how much time and energy we would have to expend to put strategies in place that address our children's behavior. If their behavior is not terribly troublesome, we are overwhelmed with other priorities at the time, and/or the effort to change the behavior would be great, then we may want to put the intervention on hold until the timing is better.

HOW TO RESPOND TO PROBLEM BEHAVIOR

Once we decide that intervention is necessary, we often wonder what we should do next. Should we ignore the behavior, try to reason with our children, impose consequences, or just get through this one instance and plan better for next time? That depends, at least in part, on our individual values, personal experiences, and beliefs about our children's behavior.

We might draw from our history, especially the way in which we were disciplined as children. We might ask advice from friends, family, or neighbors. We might seek input from medical professionals, teachers, counselors, or others who work with children. We might just wait and see, hoping that our children will grow out of it. We might consult one of the many valuable books or programs on discipline (see the Parenting Resources section in the Bibliography at the end of the book) and select strategies that sound good or appeal to us. Regardless of where we turn, it is important that we examine our logic in deciding how we will respond to our children's behavior so that we can determine which approaches will be beneficial for our children and families.

Assumptions About Behavior

It is important for us to recognize that the way we understand and deal with our children's behavior is based on attitudes, feelings, and personal assumptions regarding behavior—all of which are derived from our personal experience. Sometimes ideas about why behavior happens or how to address it are based on misconceptions or myths that have been handed down from family members, friends, or the media. Sometimes our reactions tend to be emotional, rather than rational.

We may feel responsible for absolutely everything that our children do and feel that our children's behavior is a reflection of what kind of people we are. We may believe that other people are evaluating us based on our children's behavior. We might be embarrassed, worrying about what other people will think; frustrated because our children's behavior is interfering with our plans; worried that their behavior is going to scar our children (or the rest of the family) for life; or just plain angry or sad that our children would choose to behave so badly.

Although most of the strong emotions we experience during episodes of problem behavior fade rather quickly after the behavior stops, there can still be lasting effects. We may carry traces of those feelings with us, which can change the way we see our children and prompt us to react to our children's behavior simply out of habit. Sometimes our reactions are based on certain beliefs that are not productive (e.g., discipline means punishing children; childhood should be a time for fun, not for limits; parents must be in control of their children at all times). As a result, we may respond to behavior impulsively (e.g., yelling when our children make a mistake), even though we know that those reactions are not likely to help change behavior.

Sometimes the way that we react to a particular behavior (e.g., giving in) makes it more likely that the behavior will happen again. Because we have come to expect behavior problems, we may accidentally provoke or encourage our children's difficult behavior, creating a self-perpetuating cycle. Understanding what perceptions underlie our reactions is essential to looking more objectively at behavior and developing effective solutions.

Looking at Behavior Objectively

Understanding our children's behavior (a basic feature of PBS; see Chapter 2) requires us to look *objectively* at situations and interactions, paying attention to what actually happens without becoming emotionally engaged in our children's behavior. This realistic appraisal may challenge our old assumptions and make us question our typical responses to behavior problems. Objectivity does not come naturally, particularly when we are facing behavior problems that have plagued us for a while. If, however, faulty assumptions are at the forefront of our minds while we are trying to observe and address our children's behavior, those ideas may skew our understanding of our children's behavior and therefore how we address it.

Prior to using PBS, we need to examine our assumptions and set aside any emotions or attitudes (e.g., "He's just pulling my chain") that might interfere with the process. This includes learning to ignore other people's judgments that could undermine our efforts. We also need to replace any negative self-talk with more productive, realistic perspectives. In essence, we need to find a way to get rid of our emotional baggage and open ourselves up to new beliefs about behavior.

Activity: Assumptions About Behavior

Consider situations in which your child's behavior is particularly troublesome. Write down what you think and feel about your child's behavior, and how those thoughts and feelings affect what you do in response to his or her behavior. Make a list of assumptions that may interfere with your objectivity. (Use a separate sheet of paper, if neccessary.)

_____

_____

_____

_____

_____

When we come to terms with why we understand and address behavior the way we do, we can open ourselves up to fresh perspectives and more effective ways of working with our children. We can also avoid taking situations involving problem behavior personally and therefore gain confidence and pride in how we handle such situations and ourselves.

FINDING A BETTER WAY

In our search for solutions to our children's behavior problems, we may very well find something that works or at least makes things seem better for a while. Conversely, we may find that the improvements are temporary or cause new problems to emerge that force us to go right back to the drawing board. This hit-and-miss approach can result in a lot of frustration for our children, our families, and ourselves. What we search for is real, long-term solutions to our children's behavior problems. Such an approach requires that solutions be matched to the problems and their causes—rather than focusing on getting problem behavior to stop for the time being and only in our presence, then finding out that the behavior emerges again in another situation.

PBS provides a framework for understanding and addressing behavior. It guides families and members of their support network to restructure their lives and address behavior in a way that prevents problems, teaches skills, and helps children to help themselves. It does not replace all of the other wonderful parenting strategies that have emerged over the years, but instead helps us choose the right methods for our children and families.

SUMMARY

Whether behavior is considered to be a problem depends on its impact, the circumstances in which it occurs, and the values of the people dealing with it. Addressing behavior involves careful consideration of perspectives, needs, and priorities. It is also necessary to decide whether the potential cost of addressing the behavior is worth the benefits for our children and families. When we do decide to intervene, we must try to be as objective as possible, dismissing assumptions that may interfere with the creative problem-solving that is characteristic of PBS.

Before Moving On
Have you identified your child's behaviors of concern and considered whether they are worthy of your attention (i.e., based on the Big Ds and other issues)?
Have you considered your assumptions about behavior and their impact on your responses so that you can look more objectively at your child's behavior?

CHAPTER 2

Learning About Positive Behavior Support

PBS is a research-based approach for supporting people with difficult behavior in homes, schools, and communities. This chapter provides a brief summary of the background and rationale for PBS and describes its primary features, underlying assumptions, and process. For additional information on PBS, see the numerous resources and references in the Positive Behavior Support list in the Bibliography at the end of the book.

DEFINITION

PBS has developed since the mid-1980s. It is based on the principles of applied behavior analysis, although it draws on other fields (e.g., ecological and community psychology) as well. PBS has grown beyond some earlier applications of the basic principles of behavior (e.g., behavior modification) in that it places greater emphasis on the following:

- Being proactive rather than reactive (e.g., preventing problems rather than simply relying on using consequences for behavior)

- Individualizing approaches based on the person's needs and the circumstances surrounding his or her behavior

- Respecting a person's right to make his or her own choices and participate in integrated activities

- Making plans work in everyday home, school, and community settings

PBS was originally created for children and adults with disabilities and serious behavior problems, as an alternative to the cruel and demeaning methods that were often used to manage behavior. PBS was once used mostly in highly structured school and community programs. Effective in these extreme cases, it has now been applied with a greater variety of people, to different types of behavior problems, and across a range of places. Since the late 1990s, PBS has become widely accepted for all children and is now considered a cornerstone of effective education.

Although PBS has been used successfully in schools and community programs, there has been little research studying PBS when put in place by parents themselves within typical family homes or community settings. From a common sense perspective, however, PBS may offer the greatest benefits for families and others involved in caring for and raising children. The reason

PBS makes sense for families is that it is based on basic principles that have proven to be effective, and these principles can be used in any situation, interaction, or aspect of family life.

This is particularly important because parenting is difficult, all-consuming work. In contrast to our jobs, parenting really is full time. We are on the job 24 hours per day, 7 days per week, for a lifetime. Our homes and communities are not somewhere we go or something we do but part of who we are. We know that how we address our children's behavior may not just affect our children, but possibly also our grandchildren and great-grandchildren as our philosophies are passed down from generation to generation. If we want our children to grow up to be happy and productive individuals (which, of course, we do), we need effective ways to address our children's behavior and encourage their happiness, growth, and development.

PBS is a framework and a consistent set of principles to guide how we deal with issues and select among the variety of options for structuring our homes and responding to behavior. It is an individualized, problem-solving approach. Instead of providing a standard set of procedures, it offers a flexible process for resolving the unique issues that may affect our families. It guides us to make good decisions for our families, taking into consideration our priorities and circumstances. The remaining sections of this chapter describe how PBS can apply to our families and everyday lives, including the process's grounding assumptions and primary features.

CONTEXT

PBS may best be viewed as a framework and a process for understanding behavior, structuring our homes and interactions, and resolving behavior problems. PBS is based on the assumption that if we can determine the purpose of our children's behavior and how that purpose serves them, we are in a better position to address their behavior. Consider the following scenario:

Lisa, age 9, walks into a group of adults at a block party. She begins spinning around in circles, making whirring noises, and eventually steps on someone's toes and bangs into someone else. Her parents are mortified. Why did she do that? And what should her parents do?

What if later, after talking to each other, to Lisa, and to Lisa's friends who had been with them that day, her parents determined that Lisa was still excited about a helicopter ride she had at an air show earlier that day? In addition, she was sleep deprived from the previous night's sleepover and had consumed too much sugar. Or what if her parents recognized that spinning and whirring is a game that she plays with her brother and that she is accustomed to receiving positive reactions (laughs rather than glares) when playing the game?

Knowing these things might help Lisa's parents address her behavior more effectively. For example, they might be careful not to schedule an air show and block party on the same day or might allow some time between events to let

Lisa rest and calm down. They might also decide that they need to teach Lisa that the games she plays with her brother may not be acceptable in other situations and might give her better ways to get attention from adults.

By understanding why problem behaviors occur (i.e., their purpose) and/or the situations that set the stage for behavior, we are then able to develop effective solutions. PBS therefore involves working together to understand behavior and the circumstances that affect it and finding more effective ways to prevent, teach, and respond to behavior. These solutions demonstrate respect for our children's needs and encourage our children to be more responsible for their actions.

The PBS process helps guide our decisions so that we can choose the most positive and effective methods to address our children's specific needs. Rather than supplying a cookbook of potential solutions to common problems, PBS provides a creative, problem-solving process that can be applied to many situations that we encounter as parents. In other words, it provides a roadmap for choosing among the wide array of options for dealing with behavior to which we may be exposed. To paraphrase a Chinese proverb, PBS teaches us to fish, rather than simply giving us a fish.

ASSUMPTIONS ABOUT BEHAVIOR

Some basic assumptions about behavior provide the foundation for PBS and the approach described in this book. These ideas ring true for all people and all behavior and may be especially useful when trying to understand our children and families.

First, *behavior is related to the environment in which it occurs*. People tend to behave differently in different places and situations (e.g., a library versus a party). Certain conditions allow people to perform at their best, whereas others can set the stage for people to be uncooperative, irritable, or otherwise unpleasant. For example, children often act better when they fully understand what is expected of them and are comfortable in their surroundings; conversely, some behave badly when they are distracted or presented with unrealistic demands.

Second, *all behavior has a purpose* (i.e., it allows people to get things they want or avoid things they do not want). Behavior allows people to meet their needs, either by communicating what they want to other people or by changing unpleasant circumstances themselves. People may use their behavior to get others to pay attention to them, ask for things they need, or express displeasure with a situation. For example, children may argue to get attention or procrastinate to avoid doing their chores. People continue to act in a certain way only if their behavior results in beneficial outcomes for them.

Third, *behavior is affected by physical and/or emotional conditions*. When people are ill, tired, upset, hungry, or otherwise uncomfortable, they may behave in unusual ways. For example, people may lose their tempers more readily when suffering from seasonal allergies or when under a great deal of stress. In order to behave at their best, people's medical, emotional, and personal needs must be considered and addressed.

Fourth, *behavior is influenced by broader life issues.* Things beyond what are occurring right here and now (e.g., an argument with a friend earlier in the day, an overly demanding schedule, dissatisfaction with living conditions) affect people's ability to cope with day-to-day events. Therefore, it is sometimes necessary for people to improve their lives (by changing living circumstances or relationships) to change their behavior.

Finally, *behavior changes as children mature and develop new skills.* Infants cry to get their needs met. As children learn to talk, they start to use words instead; for example, they begin asking for a toy rather than simply grabbing it. The better that children and adults can communicate their needs, deal with situations, and function more independently, the less they need to rely on other, often less suitable, means of meeting their needs. Gaining new and more appropriate strategies for dealing with difficult situations is the best way to promote behavior change.

We cannot control one another's behavior; we can only change how we structure our lives and settings and respond to the people with whom we interact. Because all of these assumptions play a part in understanding and dealing effectively with our children's behavior, we need an integrated framework to guide what we do. That is what PBS offers.

FEATURES OF POSITIVE BEHAVIOR SUPPORT

The PBS process allows us to develop a better understanding of our children's behavior so that we can make the best choices possible to address it. Keeping the preceding assumptions in mind, PBS is characterized by the following features.

Understanding Patterns

PBS involves looking objectively at children's behavior, the circumstances that may prompt the behavior to occur (e.g., the situations that seem to provoke it), and the results the behavior produces for the children (e.g., what they get or avoid because of the behavior). The importance of this approach is illustrated in the following scenario. Say that you go to the doctor because your leg is swollen and uncomfortable. Without even looking at your leg, the doctor decides to put a cast on it and tells you to stay off of it for 6 weeks. Would you trust this doctor's recommendations? A circumstance like this would be highly unusual. Doctors are expected to closely examine patients and ask them a number of questions, and only when they have a thorough understanding of the problem do they make their treatment plan.

PBS is like good diagnostic treatment. Rather than making decisions simply based on the symptoms, nature of the problem, or gut instincts, PBS is based on understanding. Gaining this understanding may require paying close attention to interactions, talking to other people who might have useful insights, and keeping a record of what is learned. In this way, PBS involves acting as detectives, looking for clues to understand children's behavior better, specifically when, where, with whom, and why children behave in certain ways.

For example, Shen might come to recognize that his children get extremely active (e.g., run around, grab and throw things around, argue with or tease each other) and do not respond to requests when they arrive home from school, hungry and tired. In reaction, Shen quickly gets his children a snack or, if things get particularly out of control, sends them to their rooms. By reacting this way, Shen is meeting his children's needs (food and/or rest). This understanding provides the basis for intervention and allows Shen to adjust particular circumstances and outcomes surrounding behavior to improve his children's behavior.

Preventing Problems

Awareness of the patterns affecting children's behavior makes it possible to change particular situations that might set the stage for our children's problem behavior and therefore make the problem behavior unnecessary. PBS involves changing things to avoid problems altogether, make difficult circumstances better, or add reminders to encourage good behavior. For example, using the pattern described in the previous section, Shen might establish some new routines, such as reviewing expectations for behavior in the car on the way home from school, having a snack ready, and/or letting his children listen to music or watch television for a little while so that they can rest when they first arrive home. These or other minor changes might avoid hassles and promote more positive interactions with and between the children.

Teaching New Skills

Although preventing problems always makes sense when possible, it is not always feasible or appropriate. PBS also involves helping children develop better ways to deal with problems and get what they need or want. Depending on the situation, this might include teaching their children skills for better communicating their needs, interacting with other people, managing their time, dealing with stress or unpleasant circumstances, or becoming more self-sufficient. For example, Shen's children's frenzied behavior when they return from school might be replaced by encouraging them to prepare their own snacks or to use relaxation skills (e.g., closing their eyes, stretching, going for a walk, writing in a journal) to recover from their busy day.

Responding Effectively

In addition to changing circumstances to prevent problems from emerging and teaching children better ways to behave, PBS also involves changing reactions to behavior so as to not inadvertently contribute to the problem. The goals are to provide consequences that reward positive behavior and to withhold outcomes (e.g., reactions, results) that may be desirable to children when they are misbehaving. In PBS, consequences are intended to teach positive behavior rather than simply stop or punish problem behavior. Consequences such as time-out, restriction, or reprimands are therefore used sparingly, if at all (see Chapter 5 for a discussion of punishment). For example, Shen could give his children the choice of a snack or some free time before starting homework if, and only if, they enter the house calmly and speak nicely to one another. If Shen is consistent in reacting this way, the payoff will be greater for positive than negative behavior.

Changing Lives

Whereas PBS does provide a framework for selecting specific strategies to resolve behavior problems, its focus and primary goal is larger than that. The overriding concern is helping children and families live more positive and productive lives. Through this process, families should be able to do more things, go to more places, and have better experiences overall. To create such a meaningful impact, people may have to make changes in broader areas, such as their relationships with one another, their daily schedules and typical routines, or their home and family arrangements. For example, to reduce problems in the afternoon, Shen may decide that he needs to decrease his children's after-school activities, enforce his children's bedtimes more consistently, monitor his children's eating habits, or change how he interacts with his children in the afternoons to improve his children's behavior.

Working Together

In order for PBS to work for children and families, everyone who is involved in the children's and families' daily lives must work together. This includes parents, teachers, baby sitters, extended family, siblings, friends, and anyone else who could have an impact on what happens with children's behavior. Working together requires open communication, the establishment of shared goals and responsibilities, and the development of sensible plans that can deal with problems wherever they occur. Working together is essential for understanding children's behavior, putting strategies in place, and making sure that the strategies work. Without collaboration, people may inadvertently undermine one another and interfere with positive changes. For example, Shen may need to communicate closely with his wife and his children's teachers in order successfully implement his strategies.

POSITIVE BEHAVIOR SUPPORT PROCESS

PBS offers a creative, problem-solving process for understanding why problem behavior occurs and how to deal with it effectively. The PBS process involves five general steps or components focused on improving our children's problem behavior and family interactions:

1. **Establishing goals:** Define the problem, which includes determining exactly what the children are doing that is of concern and the specific changes desired.

2. **Gathering information:** Watch the children's behavior and talk to other people (e.g., teachers, other family members) in order to understand why the children are behaving in this manner.

3. **Analyzing patterns:** Determine what circumstances affect the children's behavior and what they are getting or avoiding as a result of the behavior.

4. **Developing a plan:** Create strategies to prevent problems, teach the children better ways of behaving, and respond consistently to behaviors as they occur.

5. **Monitoring results:** Periodically review progress to ensure that the strategies are working and make changes as needed.

The following scenario illustrates this process.

Marcia has put off going to the grocery store for as long as she possibly can. There is no milk, bread, or cereal in the house—and nothing for dinner tonight. She starts thinking about her last few trips to the store and dread wells up inside her. There is nobody to watch Jeremy—she has to take him. Last time the scene was unbearable, forcing Marcia to leave the store in tears, dragging Jeremy, and only getting about half of the things she came to get. Marcia thinks, "If only I could grocery shop without this craziness."

Jeremy is 4 years old and the youngest of three children. He was a difficult baby—anxious, demanding, and extremely active—a pattern that continues into his childhood. He is also creative and independent. He likes to feel that he is contributing and takes pride in a job well done. As the baby in a family with two older sisters (ages 7 and 10), he is accustomed to being the focus of attention and getting his way. Any situation that limits his ability to move, explore, and exert control tends to be a problem.

Marcia decides to hope for the best, and she and Jeremy head out for the grocery store. They make it halfway down Aisle 3—and it begins: "Mommy, I want...." Jeremy's voice gets louder and whinier. Within minutes, he is grabbing things off the shelves. When Marcia tries to stop him, he pulls away and yells, "Bug off!" over and over. People pass by and look at them as if to say, "Tsk, tsk... get that child under control."

What should Marcia do? At the moment when all of this is occurring, she will probably simply manage the situation the best she can, getting what she absolutely needs and leaving the store as soon as possible. But that is not going to address the problem, and she will have to face the grocery store again. She needs a plan for next time, and the time after that. This is where PBS comes into play.

The first step in PBS is **establishing goals**. What exactly would Marcia (as well as Jeremy, other family members, and customers at the grocery store) like to happen at the store? What would a successful trip to the grocery store—or any public place—look like? What exactly are Jeremy's behaviors of concern? In considering these questions, Marcia realizes that she has modest goals. Marcia simply wants to be able to go to a store, get the items she needs, and get home without incident. It would even be nice if she and Jeremy could enjoy each other's company during these outings. Marcia imagines a successful outing: Jeremy would walk quietly next to her or maybe ride in the cart. He would keep his hands to himself, rather than taking things off shelves, running, yelling, or dropping to the floor—behaviors that have occurred during 9 out of 10 of their previous trips to the store.

These goals help to clarify Marcia and Jeremy's needs and concerns. But how can she get Jeremy to behave in the store and make this positive vision come true? That depends on why Jeremy is acting this way. What is setting him off and what is he getting out of by behaving so badly? The second step in PBS is **gathering information** in order to answer these questions. Marcia decides to start keeping a journal so that she can look more objectively at situations at the grocery store and gain a better understanding of Jeremy's behavior. She talks her concerns over with her husband and mother-in-law, who have also shopped with Jeremy and had similar experiences. When the kids are in bed and dishes are put away, Marcia takes advantage of the calm to reflect on her experiences and what her family has shared with her.

Thinking back, Marcia realizes that these types of scenes have occurred repeatedly over the past few months and are actually getting worse. She notes that Jeremy complains about having to go to the store, especially when he has to stop doing something more fun like playing with his toys or watching television. She feels that the purpose of his behavior is to deliberately shorten or stop the shopping trip so that he can resume doing something that he prefers. Typically, Marcia waits to shop until she absolutely has no choice. By the time she finally goes to the store, she needs a lot of stuff, which makes problems worse. In fact, the only good trip they have had in the past 2 months was when they needed only a few things. Marcia's current approach for dealing with Jeremy, the "hope for the best" strategy, involves saying absolutely nothing to him about shopping until they arrive at the store (in order to delay any negative reactions he may have) and then handling problems the best she can as they arise. Sometimes, when Jeremy demands things such as cookies or toys, Marcia gives in just to make peace. She is especially likely to give in if Jeremy becomes particularly demanding or disruptive. Jeremy's grandmother has taken him shopping a few times and told Marcia that her experiences have been more successful, perhaps because she has him help with the shopping.

Given this information, it is possible to start **analyzing patterns** that may be affecting Jeremy's behavior, the third step in PBS. Under what circumstances (where, when, with whom) is Jeremy's behavior best and worst? What outcomes result (what does Jeremy get or avoid) from his behavior? As Marcia looks at the information she gathered, a repeated pattern comes to mind; when on long shopping trips (purchasing more than 20 items), Jeremy demands things, grabs items off shelves, yells, and sometimes runs or throws himself down on the floor. This behavior typically results in Marcia ending the shopping trip early and/or Marcia giving in to Jeremy's demands (e.g., giving him a cookie). This leads Marcia to think that Jeremy may perform better when shopping trips are short, he knows what is expected of him, and he is allowed to help with the shopping.

Armed with this understanding, Marcia is able to start **developing a plan** for future trips to the grocery store, the fourth step in the PBS process. A PBS plan includes three types of strategies:

1. Preventing problems: Change the circumstances of grocery shopping to make it unnecessary for Jeremy to use his problem behavior.

2. Replacing behavior: Show Jeremy how to communicate his needs and/or cope with difficult situations, and remind him of appropriate behaviors as necessary.

3. Managing consequences: Change the results or outcomes of Jeremy's behavior (especially what Marcia does or says) so that he is rewarded for positive behavior and not problem behavior.

Based on her understanding, Marcia develops the following plan for Jeremy's behavior at the store:

- For the time being, take Jeremy shopping more often (e.g., twice per week) when they need fewer than 20 items.

- Explain to Jeremy why they need to shop (e.g., so there is food). Review the grocery list and expectations for Jeremy's behavior prior to going to the store and again as they arrive (e.g., "Today we need 18 items, including hamburger, cereal, and juice bars. I'd like your help finding those things. While we are in the store, I need you to walk next to me or ride in the grocery cart and to keep your voice down.").

- Ask Jeremy to get some of the things they need off the shelves and put them in the cart. Give him grocery labels or pictures of the items to help him pick out what is needed. Praise him for helping (e.g., "You found the dozen pears! Thank you for your help.").

- Encourage Jeremy to communicate more appropriately when he is bored or frustrated with shopping (e.g., saying, "How much longer do we have to shop?" or "I'm getting tired"). Respond positively to those statements by explaining what is left to do or helping him find a way to entertain himself.

- Allow Jeremy to pick one special grocery item or treat (e.g., a cookie, a balloon) that he will receive right before going to the checkout register. If he takes only what they need off the shelves, speaks quietly, and walks nicely, give him that item. Also, ask Jeremy to choose a special activity (e.g., play a favorite game, use the computer) that he may do when he gets home from the shopping trip. Make these rewards clear prior to entering the store and provide reminders of them as necessary.

• If Jeremy does raise his voice or move away from the cart, remind him of what he needs to do to earn his treat (e.g., "You need to walk quietly next to me if you want to get your cookie"). If he does not respond, take him by the hand and, if necessary, put him in the cart. Calmly explain that he will not be getting the treat this time, but he can try again next time.

• Continue to praise good behavior. Let Jeremy know that if they can finish the shopping, getting everything they need, he may still have his special activity (e.g., a favorite game or food) when he gets home. However, if Jeremy yells repeatedly or runs away, leave the store and go back later.

Marcia discusses these strategies with her husband, her other children, and her mother-in-law. Her husband and mother-in-law agree to follow the strategies and support Jeremy by encouraging his positive behavior if they are in similar situations, and her other children understand that they can support the process by helping Jeremy find grocery labels and commenting on his good behavior. Marcia promptly begins using the strategies and carries them through consistently. At the outset, Marcia feels that these strategies are "doable" most of the time, but then she realizes that she can not always shop that frequently, take that long to shop, or limit her purchases to fewer than 20 items. Therefore, she finds it necessary to have someone else watch Jeremy once in awhile so that she can shop without him.

Marcia is excited about her plan and wants to make sure it works. She decides to continue keeping her journal for **monitoring results** of the plan. This is the final step in the PBS process. In her journal, she records when they went to the store, how many items they bought, whether Jeremy helped with the shopping, whether there were any behaviors of concern, and if they were able to complete their shopping trip and get everything on their list. With this information she can objectively determine how well the plan is working and effectively find solutions to new issues as they arise. As time goes on and Jeremy improves, Marcia is able to increase the number of items she purchases and decrease the frequency of her shopping trips. She now feels comfortable going shopping with Jeremy and plans to use what she has learned in this experience with other situations (e.g., other types of stores, restaurants, amusement parks).

SUMMARY

This chapter discussed the background and features of PBS: understanding patterns, preventing problems, teaching new skills, responding effectively, changing lives, and working together. Jeremy's story provided an illustration of these primary features.

Before Moving On

 Do you understand the basic features of positive behavior support, as illustrated in Jeremy's plan?

SECTION II

The Process of Positive Behavior Support

Problem Solving Through the Process

S ection I provided an introduction to PBS—what it is and why we choose to use it while raising and interacting with our children. After reading that section, it should be apparent that PBS is not a program or standard set of procedures but an individualized *process* in which certain basic principles (i.e., understanding behavior; changing lives; working together; and using multi-element plans that include prevention, teaching, and management) can be applied to any situation. Section II describes the important elements of this problem-solving process to better understand behavior and develop effective plans for addressing it. Chapters 3, 4, 5, and 6 describe each step in the process:

Establishing goals

Gathering and analyzing information

Developing a plan

Monitoring results

For each step, detailed examples are provided. To illustrate the entire process, three children—Deon, James, and Brittany—are used as examples. These examples were developed based on the authors' collective experience in an effort to show how the process can be used with very different children, behaviors, and circumstances. A chart such as the one shown below in Table 2 follows each section and provides more information. Figure 1 provides some background information about these three children. Concise examples of the children's final behavior support plans are included in Appendix B at the end of this book.

Background Information

Deon	James	Brittany
Deon is 18 months old. He is the youngest of three brothers. Deon's mother, Adrienne, stays at home with the children and his father, Darell, is home in the evenings. Deon is bright, and energetic. He loves to look at books and be snuggled. His family is worried about Deon's whining. Whenever Adrienne tries to get things done around the house, Deon whines and clings to her. It has gotten to the point that she feels she gets nothing done.	James is 9 years old. He has one younger sister, Julie. Both of his parents (Laura and Rick) work outside of the home, but they try to keep flexible schedules that allow them to spend time with their children. James is active in sports (primarily karate) and enjoys using his free time to hang out in the neighborhood. There has been conflict between James and Julie since they were little. James yells at Julie, refuses to share his things with her, teases her, and calls her names. Sometimes he even hits, chokes, or throws things at her. More recently, James' parents have had reports of aggression with children in the neighborhood and at karate lessons. They have also noticed fewer children coming over to their house to play.	Brittany is 14 years old. She lives with her father, Nathan, who works in sales and keeps odd hours. Her grandmother, Margaret, helps care for her when Nathan is gone. Brittany attends high school and a recreational after-school program. She enjoys learning about and discussing outer space. Brittany has a developmental disability (Asperger syndrome) that affects how she understands and deals with social situations. Although she does well in most academic subjects, she dislikes physical activities (e.g., chores) and only talks about things of interest to her (e.g., outer space). When pressured to do things she does not like or to talk about other topics, Brittany begins repeating facts or humming loudly, which draws negative attention to her and sets her apart from her peers.

Figure 1. Background information on the three example children.

CHAPTER 3

Establishing Goals

The first step in the PBS process is for us to clarify our goals for our children, families, and lives. We need to ask ourselves questions such as

- "What is going on that we find to be a problem?"
- "What changes do we envision for our children and families?"
- "What outcomes would makes us feel successful?"

The purpose of this chapter is to help us answer these questions and get a clear picture of what we want to achieve, which will then launch us into the next steps of the process—understanding and addressing our children's behavior.

DEFINING BEHAVIORS OF CONCERN

An important first step in understanding our children's behavior is to define the specific actions that we are finding to be a problem. By defining behavior, we clarify exactly what types of behavior are going on, which can help us determine what we want to change. We may be asking ourselves, "Why define the behavior? I know it when I see it." When the behavior is defined, we can

1. Look at the behavior *objectively.* That means being able to observe and consider the behavior without prejudice or emotions getting in the way.

2. Be more consistent when trying to understand and address behavior.

3. Facilitate communication among everyone interacting with our children.

Children's behavior should be defined in terms of what they say or do. The description of their behavior needs to be specific enough that everyone involved with our children can immediately recognize the behavior when it occurs. For example, although many people may label a behavior as disrespectful, the specific behaviors they associate with that label may vary considerably (e.g., talking back to adults, ignoring authority figures, calling others names). For such labels to be useful in understanding and responding to children's behavior adequately, we need to define more specifically what we mean.

In summary, a well-defined behavior

- Describes what the behavior looks like (e.g., the child stamps his or her feet and walks away)
- Describes what the behavior sounds like (e.g., the child makes a loud, high-pitched squeal)

- Includes typical examples of the behavior (e.g., the child often calls people, "Stupid")
- Avoids using behavior descriptions with unclear meanings (e.g., "The child argues and insults parents, teachers, and coaches" instead of "The child sasses adults")

Figure 2 lists behaviors of concern for the three children being used as examples.

Behaviors of Concern		
Deon	**James**	**Brittany**
Whining: high-pitched "eh" sound or repetitive requests like "up, up"	Yelling: speaking with a raised voice	Avoiding: refusal to participate in physical activities, conversations, or household chores, by ignoring the task at hand or by continuing to engage in other activities (e.g., reading a schoolbook, talking obsessively about outer space when the ongoing conversation is about other things)
Clinging: grabbing and holding people around legs, or pulling on their clothing	Teasing: calling others names such as, "fat-face" or "crybaby," making threats such as, "I'll give your toy to the garbage man," or taking things away from smaller children and holding them out of reach	
	Hurting others: hitting or kicking objects or people; choking people	

Figure 2.   Behaviors of concern for the three example children.

 ## Activity: Defining Behavior

What does your child *say* or *do* that concerns you? Describe the behavior clearly, providing examples as needed.

_____

_____

_____

_____

_____

ESTABLISHING BROADER GOALS

It is important to not only identify the behaviors of concern, but also to consider the broader goals we would like to achieve through our efforts. When we are asked what our goals are, we might initially say things like

- "Get him to stop hitting and teasing his sister!"

- "Get her to stop yelling at me when I ask her to do things."

- "Get them to stop hanging all over me when I'm trying to have a conversation."

Why is it so important for us to address our children's behavior? What changes would we ultimately like to see in our children's lives? What are our broader goals for our children and how might changing our children's behavior help them to achieve those goals? PBS encourages us to go beyond stopping a problem behavior and come up with some broader goals that will improve the overall quality of our children's and families' lives. Broader goals might relate to the following:

- Improving children's overall health or emotional state (e.g., happiness)

- Making it possible for children to go to more places or do more things (e.g., being able to attend birthday parties unsupervised, being able to sleep over at a friend's house)

- Giving children more opportunities to make their own choices (e.g., selecting their own educational courses, preparing their own snacks)

- Enhancing or expanding children's friendships and other personal relationships (e.g., improving ability to communicate and interact with peers)

- Improving family life in general (e.g., being able to visit public places without any behavior disruptions)

Everyone who interacts with our children on a regular basis should be involved in establishing these types of goals. This is because parents, family members, teachers, and coaches are better able to identify the children's needs and goals of importance and to promote shared responsibility and commitment to supporting the children's achievement if they work collectively. One of the best ways to identify goals, especially those for children with complicated needs (e.g., medical problems, significant disabilities requiring a variety of therapies and supports) or complex family or school circumstances (e.g., foster care, shared custody, educational services in multiple settings), is to use a process called person-centered planning. In this process, the child and everyone involved in his or her life gets together and, using large paper and colored markers, outlines the child's strengths, needs, current circumstances, goals for the future, and steps toward those goals. Because person-centered planning directly involves the child, family, friends, and support providers in the process, it tends to help encourage a shared vision and commitment to the goals. (See the Parenting Resources section in the Bibliography at the end of the book for references on person-centered planning.)

Working together to identify goals builds unity among the people involved in our children's lives, and creating a positive vision for our children's future provides hope and a sense of direction. The result is that we are more optimistic and motivated to make the necessary changes and improve the lives of ourselves and our children both in the short term and in the long-ranging future. Figure 3 provides broad goals for the three example children.

Broad Goals		
Deon	**James**	**Brittany**
Deon will play by himself for 10 minutes (while Adrienne cooks dinner, talks on the telephone, and so forth). Adrienne will be able to do some of the things she wants to do on a daily basis (e.g., have conversations with friends, take a shower).	James will be able to play with Julie or with children in the neighborhood without supervision. James's relationships with his sister and his peers will improve (e.g., peers will be willing to come to James's house, James will be able to play with Julie without making her cry). James will continue to be involved in karate and other sports.	Brittany will have dinner with Nathan each night and complete a couple of basic chores. Brittany will participate in more (e.g., 4 out of 5) after-school activities at the recreation center and in the community. Brittany will have conversations with others about topics other than outer space every day.

Figure 3. Broad goals for the three example children.

Activity: Setting Goals

List a few of the most important broad goals you would like to achieve. Consider goals for your child as an individual and as a member of your family.

1. _____

_____

2. _____

_____

3. _____

_____

FINDING A STARTING POINT

It is often helpful for us to begin the PBS process by determining approximately how often, how long, or how serious our children's behaviors of concern are currently occurring. Establishing these initial estimates of the behavior gives a clear starting point for making comparisons after the strategies have been put in place. Later on, we will be able to say with some confidence that our children's behavior has improved or that the plan has been effective (e.g., the child's refusal to do what he or she is told has diminished from approximately 20 times per day to fewer than 3 times per day).

To gather this information about our children's behavior before the PBS process has begun, we want to use the simplest method possible that will give us a useful estimate of how long or how difficult our children's behavior is. Using the definitions for our children's behavior that we developed earlier, we can use one of the following options:

1. Counting the behavior (i.e., frequency): making a note each time the children do the behavior (e.g., tally how many times each day the children refuse to follow directions or tease their peers or siblings)

2. Timing the behavior (i.e., duration): recording how long a behavior goes on (e.g., note how long the children cry or take to do a chore)

3. Rating the seriousness of behavior (i.e., magnitude): using some kind of scale (e.g., a number between 1 and 5), estimate how bad the behavior was (e.g., a Level-4 tantrum)

If it seems too difficult, awkward (e.g., disruptive to the family) or time consuming for us to consistently use these methods but we still want to get a baseline of our children's behavior, we can limit our record-keeping to short periods each day (i.e., sampling). For example, we might just pay attention to what happens at the dinner table, rating how mealtime went (see Figure 4 for other examples).

Activity: Tracking Behavior

Design a simple way to determine how often or how long your child is engaging in the behaviors you have defined as being a problem. Use the counting, timing, or rating methods as appropriate.

_____

_____

_____

_____

Methods of Tracking Behavior		
Deon	**James**	**Brittany**
Adrienne decides to focus on preparing dinner and to estimate what percent of the time Deon spends whining. On a typical day, Deon whines for long periods, almost half of the time Adrienne spends preparing dinner, and clings to her for nearly the whole time.	James's parents keep a log of every time he hurts or tries to hurt Julie. The log also includes any reports from the karate instructor or the neighborhood children and their parents. James's parents find that on the average, James's yelling and teasing happen five to six times per day, and he tends to hurt others twice per day.	Nathan, Brittany's teachers, and the recreation center supervisor write down Brittany's schedule for her reference. Brittany records which activities she participates in, with whom she interacts, and the topics of conversation. Brittany participates in one out of five nonacademic activities at school, two out of five activities at the recreation center, and about half of required activities at home. She interacts with two people per day, with the conversations almost always on the topic of outer space.

Figure 4. Methods of tracking behavior for the three example children.

SUMMARY

Behavior is anything that a person says or does. When we are able to describe our children's behavior clearly and objectively, we can clarify what is going on and focus on the problem. When we understand the problem clearly, we can begin to think about our goals for our children. This will probably include short-term goals (e.g., "stop hitting") but should also include long-term and broader goals that will improve our children's (and our families') lives.

Before Moving On
Have you defined your child's behavior clearly?
Have you considered broader goals you would like to achieve?

CHAPTER 4

Gathering and Analyzing Information

Once we have a vision for the future and know what we want to achieve, including identifying our children's specific behaviors of concern and deciding on broader goals, the next step is to gather information and gain a better understanding of what is affecting our children's behavior and the circumstances surrounding it. Information gathering is important because what we learn about our children's behavior sets the course for developing solutions that will best fit our children, families, and lives. If we have a good understanding of what our children are doing and why, we are much more likely to come up with solutions that will work.

The purpose of gathering information is for us to figure out what is affecting our children's behavior. This does not mean collecting complex data through fancy charts, clipboards, and tape recorders. Information gathering essentially involves looking at what is happening when the problem behavior occurs, and noting the situations in which it does not occur. We need to focus on two main things:

What is going on before the behavior

What happens after the behavior

When trying to understand what happens **before** our children's behavior, we need to consider the "Four Ws." The primary focus is on gathering information from the circumstances that happen right before the problem behavior or that seem to prompt the problem behavior to occur.

1. **W**ho is around when the behavior happens (e.g., siblings, friends, teachers, parents, pets, neighbors)?

2. **W**hat are the demands, expectations, or typical activities that occur when the behavior happens (e.g., playing with friends, doing chores, completing school work)?

3. **W**here does the behavior occur (e.g., at home, in a public place)?

4. **W**hen does the behavior occur (e.g., before breakfast, during extracurricular activities, in the evening, after friends leave)?

Sometimes problem behavior is related to things that happen or conditions that exist long before the behavior. Such events can set children up for good or bad behavior. Examples of more distant events or circumstances that can influence behavior are physical conditions (e.g., hunger, thirst, illness, medication effects, tiredness) and major events (e.g., a change in the regular schedule, a fight with a friend or family member, a general dissatisfaction with daily activities). These types of conditions or events can have an effect on children's overall behavior, making them react more strongly to things that happen to them.

Another important piece of information is what happens to children **after** a problem behavior—the *consequences*. Often when people talk about consequences, they are referring to punishment, such as time-out or withdrawing a privilege. This book uses a broader meaning of the term consequences and considers it everything that occurs following the behavior—every outcome, reaction, or result. This definition includes how parents, peers, and other adults respond, both purposefully and inadvertently, when children behave in a particular way. What happens after behavior is very important because it helps us to understand what goal is being fulfilled by the behavior—that is, what children are getting or avoiding when they use that behavior. For example, some behaviors may be used to gain attention, while other behaviors may allow them to get toys, activities, or other things they want. Other behaviors may be focused on children avoiding things they do not like, such as the planned consequences for their misbehavior.

HOW TO GATHER INFORMATION

To get a clear picture of the circumstances surrounding our children's behavior, we need to do some detective work: gathering information and looking for clues. In this process, we want to take advantage of what other people know and find out what happens in various places and situations throughout the day. Scientists and specially trained educators use sophisticated methods of collecting information (or data). Gathering information to better understand our children's behavior, however, does not have to be formal. There are simple ways to collect information. They include three general methods: watching, talking, and recording. Blank information-gathering tools that tend to be useful in many different circumstances are included in Appendix B at the end of this book for frequent photocopying.

Watching

It may seem obvious, but the best way for us to develop an understanding about our children's problem behavior may be to simply watch them. The trick is to watch them objectively, rather than allowing preconceived notions to affect our perceptions. We need to pay attention and take note of what is happening around our children's behavior in all the different situations and places that might be relevant. This means noticing the times our children behave appropriately as well as the times when they do not and considering who is present during those times, what is happening around our children, where our children are, and what time of day it is. It may help to write down some of what they notice when watching (see the Recording section later in this chapter for more details).

Activity: Watching

Think of some situations in which your child 1) behaves well and 2) has behavior problems. Watch your child, taking note of everything you see and hear and keeping the who, what, where, when, and why questions in your mind as you observe.

1. _____

_____

_____

2. _____

_____

_____

Talking

One of the simplest ways to gather information about our children's behaviors of concern is to talk to other people. Talking about concerns and listening to the input of others can allow us to better understand our own perceptions and develop fresh ideas. Obviously, the most important people we can talk to are our children. When we take the time to listen carefully, even young children can offer essential insights into their behavior, although they are often not able to understand or clearly express their feelings in relation to their behavior. We can also talk to our family members, our children's friends, and anyone else who is familiar with our children's behavior (e.g., teachers and baby sitters).

During these discussions, we can explore behavior patterns, considering the Four Ws and other possible things that could be affecting our children's behavior, including distant events or conditions of which we are aware. These discussions may help us recall what events or consequences happened right after our children's behavior. It may be helpful to write down the things we discover through these discussions. Sometimes it is easier to find a pattern when the ideas are down on paper. A copy of the Interviewing questions is included as the Interview Record in Appendix B at the end of this book for frequent photocopying.

Activity: Interviewing

Talk to your child and/or someone who knows your child well. Ask this person the following questions about the problem behavior, asking additional questions until you fully understand his or her perspective.

What are _____ greatest strengths and interests? (e.g., What does _____ do well, enjoy?)

_____

_____

What specifically is _____ doing that is of concern to you?

_____

_____

Under what circumstances (when, where, with whom) do these behaviors occur most?

_____

_____

Under what circumstances (when, where, with whom) do these behaviors occur least?

_____

_____

What do you think _____ gets or avoids through these behaviors?

_____

_____

Is there anything else you think might be affecting _____ behavior?

_____

_____

Recording

As mentioned earlier in this chapter, recording observations or discussions with others can be a useful way to keep track of the information collected. Recording the information can also help us look more objectively at what we are discovering, which will improve our understanding of our children's behavior. We can record the information with simple methods such as keeping notes of what happens each day or more elaborate methods like tracking specific details about behavior (e.g., when, how often, how long).

Keeping a journal is an especially good way to gather information if we do not have another person with whom we can discuss the problem. When using a journal, we simply write down what we remember about our children's behaviors whenever there is an opportunity to reflect on them (e.g., each night after the child goes to bed). An example of a journal entry recording Brittany's behavior follows:

Monday, January 5—I picked Brittany up from her after-school program and came home after a long day at work. The program supervisor told me that Brittany had refused to participate in any of the activities that day—again. When we got home, she went directly to her room. She stayed there until I asked her to come out and help me set the table. She said she needed to finish the part she was reading and refused to come out. After asking her to come out three more times, I took the book away. She then lay down on her bed and started to cry and hum loudly. I ended up setting the table and eating by myself. It seems like she wants to do less every day. I want her to have friends and take part in life.

Some other formats for recording include simple checklists and more complete behavior logs. Checklists require us to list the behaviors of concern and then make a notation every time the behaviors occur. For example, Figure 5 shows how James's parents might tally every time James teases Julie during a particular activity (e.g., homework).

We also might want to know how long behaviors occur. For example, Figure 6 illustrates how Deon's parents might record what time Deon goes to sleep at night, what time he wakes up in the morning, and how long his naps last so they can determine how much sleep he needs to be fully rested and therefore how sleep affects the frequency of his whining. We can also record behavior in a way that helps us pinpoint the times of day our children's behavior is most and least likely to be challenging. With this system, we can simply

---

Number of times James teases Julie while they do their homework:

11/15	III
11/16	IIIII III
11/17	IIII

Figure 5. Example tally sheet for James recording how often his behaviors occur.

Date	Time asleep	Time awake	Nap	Notes
4/4	9:30 P.M.	4:15 A.M.	2½ hours	Ate very little Whined throughout about half of the dinner preparation time
4/5	8:00 P.M.	6:45 A.M.	2 hours	Busy day, ate well Able to be redirected to an activity when he began whining before dinner
4/6	10:15 P.M.	6:00 A.M.	3½ hours	Friends over until 9:30 P.M. Whined continuously throughout the dinner preparation

Figure 6. Example chart for Deon recording how long his behaviors occur.

mark whether a behavior occurs within a particular period of time. Using this information, we can narrow down when to look more closely at our children's behavior and the circumstances around their behavior. For example, Figure 7 shows the times of day when Deon whines (the shaded boxes signify the times). Deon's parents might want to focus on, and possibly gather more in-

Deon's Whining							
Time	S	M	T	W	R	F	S
7:00 A.M.–8:00 A.M.	▓			▓		▓	
8:00 A.M.–9:00 A.M.		▓		▓			
9:00 A.M.–10:00 A.M.				▓			
10:00 A.M.–11:00 A.M.							
11:00 A.M.–12:00 P.M.		▓		▓			
12:00 P.M.–1:00 P.M.		▓		▓			
1:00 P.M.–2:00 P.M.							
2:00 P.M.–3:00 P.M.							
3:00 P.M.–4:00 P.M.			▓				
4:00 P.M.–5:00 P.M.					▓		
5:00 P.M.–6:00 P.M.	▓			▓	▓	▓	
6:00 P.M.–7:00 P.M.			▓				
7:00 P.M.–8:00 P.M.							

Figure 7. Example chart for Deon recording the times of day when behavior is most and least likely to be challenging. Shaded boxes show times when the behavior occurred.

formation on, the early morning, mid-day, and just prior to dinner times. A blank chart for recording times of behavior is included in Appendix B at the end of this book for frequent photocopying.

We also need to capture more information than just whether the behavior occurs. We may want to record information so that we can look closely at what is going on around our children's behavior. Behavior logs are especially useful because the logs allow us to easily identify behavior patterns, which can lead to a better understanding of behavior. Behavior logs involve recording when the behavior occurs and what happens before and after the behavior. Figure 8 is an example of a behavior log for James. A blank copy of the Behavior Log is included in Appendix B at the end of this book for frequent photocopying.

BEHAVIOR LOG		
Name: James Date: August		
Situation: Interactions with Julie and peers		
What happened before	**What he did**	**What happened after**
8/15 3:05 P.M. While riding home from school, Julie asked James some questions about the handheld videogame he was playing.	James yelled at Julie, "Get out of my face! I'm trying to play a game here!"	Julie laughed. Laura told him if he didn't stop yelling she would take the videogame away.
8/16 5:15 P.M. The neighborhood children were playing kickball in the cul-de-sac outside our house. One of the smaller boys kicked the ball the wrong way.	James picked up the ball and flung it at the boy, hitting him in the face.	The boy started to cry and left the game. Two other boys followed him, calling James a jerk.
8/18 6:30 P.M. While at the dinner table, Julie was talking about a movie she and James had watched earlier.	James interrupted Julie three times to correct her explanation.	Julie screamed at James, "Shut up!" Rick told him to be quiet and let Julie explain it her way.
	James yelled, "She's always getting me in trouble!"	Rick threatened to make James leave the table. Rick tried to explain that it wasn't Julie's fault; it was James's fault.

Figure 8. Example behavior log recording more detailed information for James's behavior.

Activity: Behavior Log

Select a time when your child's behavior is consistently difficult. Practice recording what your child says or does and what occurs before and after his or her behavior in that situation.

What happened before	What he or she did	What happened after

The behavior log provides a lot of important information, but it also takes more time to complete and may be more difficult to interpret. Working with a checklist first may help us to pinpoint the times of the day problem behaviors are most likely to occur, making it possible for us to focus our recordings on those more intense times.

In addition to gathering information ourselves, we can ask other people (e.g., teachers) to pay attention to and possibly record behaviors they notice. Strategies for keeping a record of our children's behavior should be selected (or designed) based on our needs and circumstances. The strategies should not be time-consuming or difficult, or we will not use them consistently. The strategies also should focus on the things about which we are most concerned. Figure 9 provides some ideas for strategies for the three children in the case examples:

Examples of Information Gathering		
Deon	**James**	**Brittany**
Watching: before meals, during telephone calls, and whenever Adrienne is not busy

Talking: to Darell, to Deon's older siblings, and to Deon's baby sitter | Watching: during play times with Julie and peers

Talking: to James, to Julie, to the mothers in the carpool, and to James's karate instructor

Recording: what James and the other children were doing when fights occurred, what happened after James's acts of aggression | Talking: to Brittany, to the recreational program supervisor, to Brittany's special education teacher, and to Brittany's other teachers

Recording: the number of activities Brittany does each day and people she interacts with each day |

Figure 9. Examples of information gathering for the three example children.

Activity: Information Gathering

Think about what information might be useful in trying to understand your child's behavior and develop a plan for watching (when? where?), talking (to whom?), and recording (in what manner?).

Watching _____

_____

_____

Talking _____

_____

_____

Recording _____

_____

_____

ANALYZING PATTERNS

Once we have gathered enough information on our children's behavior and the circumstances surrounding our children's behavior, we are ready for the third step in this process—analyzing patterns or making sense of what we know. How much information is enough? We need to gather information until we can begin to see patterns. The term patterns refers to repeated or consistent sequences of events across situations and over time. We know we are starting to understand patterns when we can begin to predict when behaviors are likely to occur or what events tend to follow our children's behavior. We want to be confident about patterns, which means we need to have a lot of evidence to support the patterns and very little to prove the patterns incorrect.

Finding Patterns

Using the information we have gathered, we need to look for patterns. To identify these patterns, we should ask ourselves these questions:

1. Under what conditions (where, with whom, when, during what activities) is the behavior most likely to happen? When is it least likely to happen?

2. What typically happens as a result of the behavior (e.g., outcomes, reactions, consequences)? What does the behavior achieve or avoid for the child?

Basically, we want to know what purposes our children's behavior serves for them and what situations seem to cause the problem behavior to occur.

To come to these conclusions, we may need to go over everything we have learned, rethinking past discussions and looking through the records. We might want to sit down with our families and others who play an important role in our children's lives and work together to think of possible patterns. Together, we can make a list of things that are most likely and least likely to predict behavior problems. It may be helpful to make some guesses about what our children get or avoid through their behavior and then try to identify examples that support (or challenge) those guesses.

If we have been recording, one technique for identifying patterns is to color-code the journals or logs. Using three different-colored markers or highlighters, we can clearly denote anything that happened before the behavior in one color, the behavior itself in another color, and what happened after the behavior in a third color. This can make it easier to identify those situations, people, or activities that can influence the problem behavior. Figure 10 identifies patterns for the three children in the case examples.

Patterns of Behavior

Deon	James	Brittany
Whining is most likely to occur: during meal preparation; amid transitions (e.g., getting ready to leave house); in busy, crowded, or unfamiliar places; when Adrienne is paying attention to someone or something else (speaking on the telephone, speaking with a friend, doing household chores).	Teasing is most likely to occur: at home with Julie when they are left together for more than 15 minutes, during unstructured games when James is socializing with younger children.	Avoiding is most likely to occur: when Brittany has been alone for a while, was engrossed in a book, or was on the Internet and is asked to do something else (e.g., a chore); when expectations for social interaction are high (e.g., girls her own age are talking casually).
Whining is least likely to occur: at bath or bed time, when someone is playing or snuggling with Deon.	Teasing is least likely to occur: when James is socializing with older children, during class periods at school.	Avoiding is least likely to occur: when other people take the lead in conversations; when her routine is clearly defined.
The result of the behavior: Adrienne stops what she is doing to reprimand him or direct him to other activity, giving him undivided attention.	The result of the behavior: James is sent to his room, spanked, or punished in other ways; the teased children give him a reaction (e.g., Julie yells, threatens him, or sobs hysterically; if she tries to fight back, the problems escalate and James becomes aggressive); James is told to sit out during karate; smaller children avoid James.	The result of the behavior: Brittany avoids doing chores and interacting with other people, is able to continue her favorite activities.

Figure 10.   Patterns of behavior for the three example children.

It is important to realize that some behaviors can have more than one purpose or function. For example, Deon might whine to avoid unpleasant (i.e., busy, chaotic) situations. He may use the same behavior to get Adrienne's attention and affection. We need to make sure that all possible purposes have been examined, because they will need to look at and plan for these situations differently (e.g., figuring out what is unpleasant about certain situations and changing these things, figuring out how and when Deon gets attention from Adrienne).

Activity: Finding Patterns

Identify circumstances in which your child's problem behavior is most likely or least likely to occur (the Four Ws) and consider what they seem to get or avoid as a result of that behavior.

Behavior is...	Most likely	Least likely
When		
Where		
With whom		
What activities		

What do the behaviors...	Get	Avoid

We need to remember the broader issues. In addition to the immediate events preceding and following our children's behavior, we may feel that some broader conditions or more distant events are affecting their behavior. As mentioned before, these other influences might include the following:

- Medical conditions (e.g., irritations provoked by allergy problems result in the child becoming less tolerant of a sibling's behavior)

- Overall activity patterns (e.g., stresses over extensive homework or extra-curricular activities lead to the child crying and complaining when he or she is asked to join in on family events)

- Personal relationships (e.g., a new friendship improves the child's demeanor and willingness to help out around the house)

We should identify these conditions and events so that we can consider them when planning strategies to address our children's behavior.

Summarizing What Is Known

Sometimes it is helpful for us to summarize what we know about circumstances that affect our children's behavior and the purpose(s) their behavior serves in a phrase, sentence, or short paragraph. The summary should include what seems to prompt our children's behavior, what exactly our children say or do, and what occurs (what our children get or avoid) as a result of the behavior. The following summary statements would be suitable for the children in the three case examples:

- When Adrienne tries to do something other than interact with Deon (e.g., talk to someone in person or on the telephone, make dinner, read a magazine), he whines, clings to her leg, and repeatedly asks to be picked up. This usually results in Adrienne talking to him, trying to soothe him, and eventually stopping what she is doing to focus entirely on him. This behavior is more likely to occur when the environment is chaotic or if Deon is around unfamiliar people. His behavior gets even worse when he is hungry, tired, or sick.

- When James is playing or interacting with younger children in less structured situations for lengthy periods (i.e., more than 15 minutes), he yells, refuses to share things, calls the children names, and teases them. If the children try to defend themselves or do something he sees as wrong (e.g., use a toy incorrectly, make a mistake while playing a game), he hits, kicks, or throws things at them. The children cry, which James seems to enjoy. James's parents and other authority figures provide consequences (e.g., spank him, send him to his room, make him stop playing) but these consequences do not have an effect on his behavior. James does not do these things at school or with children who are bigger and older than he is.

- When Nathan or the school counselors ask Brittany to participate in physical activities (e.g., chores around the house, games at school) or to talk with her peers on topics other than outer space, she refuses to do as she is told, ignores them, or talks obsessively about outer space. If they pressure her, she cries or hums loudly. They usually end up just giving in (and letting her do as she pleases) which allows her to avoid certain activities and social interactions. Brittany is more resistant to participating in activities when she has to stop doing something she likes, the situation is socially demanding, or the expectations are unclear.

Activity: Summarizing Patterns

Write a sentence or short paragraph to describe the patterns in your child's behavior. Identify more than one pattern as necessary.

When _____

occurs, my child does _____

to get/avoid _____ .

In a perfect world, we would be completely sure that the patterns we relate to our children's problem behavior are correctly identified. In reality, it is sometimes hard to be sure. Therefore, it may be helpful for us to test our hypotheses (or best guesses), provided that doing so will not put our children or others at risk. We can set up situations we think might affect our children's behavior and see if our children's behavior in the situations is the behavior we expected. Figure 11 gives examples of how hypotheses might be tested. Our beliefs about these patterns will also be confirmed—or challenged—when we put our strategies in place. If the interventions work, our hypotheses were correct; if not, we may have overlooked something and need to investigate the problem behavior more closely, returning to the gathering information stage.

SUMMARY

Chapter 3 taught us to define behavior objectively and establish broader goals for our children. Chapter 4 guided us in how to gather information through talking, watching, and recording; and how to identify patterns surrounding our children's behavior. With this knowledge (and the greater sensitivity to

Ways to Test Hypotheses		
Deon	**James**	**Brittany**
Adrienne could withhold her attention when Deon whines and see what his reaction is. For example, does he whine louder or stop whining?	James's parents could ask Julie to walk away from James when he teases her, rather than react to James's teasing, and see if this new response has an effect on his behavior.	Brittany's counselor could ask Brittany to leave her books in her backpack during activity time and see if this encourages Brittany to participate more.

Figure 11. Ways to test hypotheses for the three example children's behavior.

our children's needs that tends to accompany this knowledge), we can begin to develop behavior interventions that are more likely to be successful.

Before Moving On

 Have you gathered enough information through talking, watching, and recording to understand what is affecting your child's behavior?

 Have you identified patterns that include what increases or decreases the likelihood of your child's behavior and what consequences he or she gets or avoids as a result of the behavior?

CHAPTER 5

Developing a Plan

The most important lesson thus far in this book is that we must understand our children's behavior before we can begin to address it effectively. That means knowing the triggers and motivations behind the behavior. After completing Chapters 3 and 4, we should have a good understanding of

- What exactly our children do or say that concerns us, and what behavior we would like our children to do instead

- Which circumstances provoke our children's best and worst behavior

- What purpose might our children's behavior be serving (what our children get or avoid as a result of their behavior)

Armed with this information, we can come up with plans to improve our children's behavior and, hopefully, to improve our children's lives in general. The focus of PBS is not to try to control children but to influence their behavior by organizing our environments and by approaching and responding to our children differently. Therefore, our plans will be made up of strategies based on the patterns we have identified and will involve changing our own behavior. The overriding goal is to promote positive behavior so that our children no longer need to use their problem behavior to achieve their wants and needs and negotiate their circumstances. Integrating all the information and strategies identified in the previous chapters into an overall behavior support plan can be very helpful with regard to capturing and organizing the strategies selected and maintaining consistency in implementation. A blank behavior support plan is included in Appendix A at the end of this book for frequent photocopying. This chapter gives details on three general strategies we can use to address our children's behavior based on the understanding gained from Chapter 2:

1. Preventing problems by changing circumstances that provoke problem behavior (e.g., avoiding things that trigger problems)

2. Replacing behaviors of concern with other, more positive behaviors that help children communicate their needs and cope with difficult situations more effectively and appropriately

3. Managing consequences or outcomes so that children are rewarded for positive behavior and are not inadvertently rewarded for problem behavior

To provide a broad overview of these plan elements, Figure 12 is a summary of the strategies for Jeremy (the child described in Chapter 2) based on

Strategies in Jeremy's Plan		
When problems occur: During extended trips to the grocery store, when Marcia failed to make expectations for his behavior clear to him, when he is left out of shopping activities	Behaviors of concern: Demanding things, grabbing unnecessary items from the grocery shelves, yelling and running in and around the store	Purposes of behavior: To make Marcia give in to his demands (i.e., giving him a treat or toy he has demanded), to make the shopping trip end early
Preventing problems: Go to the store more frequently so that fewer items may be needed per trip, thus making each trip shorter. Review with Jeremy the behaviors that are expected of him and the items on the grocery list before going to store (also remind him of these expectations just before entering store).	Replacing behavior: Encourage Jeremy to communicate in a polite manner when he is bored or tired of shopping (e.g., "How much longer do we need to be here?" instead of throwing a temper tantrum). Have Jeremy help with the shopping by giving him labels or pictures of the items he can pick out himself. Have Jeremy practice the behaviors that are expected before and during trips to the grocery store (i.e., stay next to his mother or sit in the cart, keep his voice down).	Managing consequences: Praise Jeremy for following the expectations. Allow Jeremy to pick a treat at the check-out counter and do a special activity when he gets home, but only if he has used appropriate behavior. When Jeremy raises his voice or moves away from the cart, remind him of how he should behave. If Jeremy does not respond to the reminder, take him by the hand and put him in the cart, letting him know that he lost his privilege of getting a check-out treat but that he can still have his special activity when they get home. If Jeremy still continues to behave inappropriately, leave the store and come back later.

Figure 12.   Summary of the strategies in Jeremy's plan.

the patterns identified. The remainder of this chapter explains and illustrates these strategies using Deon, James, and Brittany as examples.

PREVENTING PROBLEMS

When we know with some degree of certainty what specific situations and conditions provoke our children's problem behavior, we may be able to prevent some problems just by changing these circumstances. Basically, we can plan certain preventive strategies by answering the following question: "What particular situations can I change to prevent my child's problem behavior and encourage positive behavior?"

Avoiding Bad Situations Altogether

Changing situations to prevent problems can be done in different ways. One option is to simply avoid bad situations altogether. This means shielding children from certain experiences and/or better meeting their needs so that unnecessary discomfort does not prompt problem behavior. Some examples follow:

- If our children have problems with certain places, people, or activities—and involvement with these people and things are not absolutely essential—we can refrain from making our children have contact with them (e.g., letting your teenager decide not to attend your office parties, serving peas at dinnertime instead of creamed spinach).

- If our children are more likely to misbehave when they are sick, tired, or hungry, we can address those needs (e.g., limiting exposure to irritating allergens, making sure to allow time for naps and relaxation) and/or avoid doing activities that the children dislike or find difficult during those times.

- If our children's problem behavior occurs when they want attention, we can give them unconditional, one-to-one attention at specific times throughout the day (e.g., asking children about their day upon return from school, snuggling each child at bedtime).

- If our children misbehave when they have to give up things or stop doing activities they like, we can work to make sure they have enough time to do those activities (e.g., making sure the child can play outside at least an hour every day, setting aside a certain amount of time for watching television).

For us to avoid difficult situations for our children is sensible and an important way to show respect for our children's needs. It may not, however, always be possible (e.g., children really do need to brush their teeth and help with household chores).

Making Difficult Circumstances Better

A second option is for us to make difficult circumstances better. We can make particular situations more enjoyable by adding (or embedding) something our children like in those situations. For example, if our children's problem behavior occurs only during certain activities, we can change aspects of those activities to make them more pleasurable (e.g., shorten or simplify a chore, allow the children to listen to music while doing a chore, include a friend to help with doing a chore). If our children misbehave when our attention is focused elsewhere, we can give them something fun to do while waiting (e.g., read a book, play a handheld video game). If problems occur when we ask our children to stop doing an enjoyable activity, we can involve them in the transition (e.g., have the children turn off the computer themselves) and/or let them know when they can continue the enjoyable activity again. And if our children act inappropriately when we confront them, we can change the manner in which we correct or make requests to our children.

One important consideration to take note of is the way in which we communicate with our children during difficult situations—not only what we say, but also the tone, body language, and expressions that we use. Styles of communication can elicit from children cooperation and pleasant interactions or resistance and negative behavior. For example, Table 2 lists interactions that may help or hinder communication with children.

A particularly effective strategy to prevent problems and encourage positive behavior is for us to offer our children more choices and the freedom to make their own decisions, thus allowing them more personal control. If we take the time to really think about it, we may realize that there are many areas in which we make decisions for our children that our children could be making for themselves—and that this may be contributing to our children's behavior. Providing opportunities for children to make choices builds independence and fosters good decision-making skills. Examples include allowing children to

- Pick which of several household chores to do first
- Decide how they want to arrange their room
- Determine the order of activities for the day
- Decide what clothing and jewelry they will wear
- Choose between menu options for dinner
- Select the friends with whom they will play
- Say "no" to requests

Table 2. Examples of interactions that help and hinder communication with children

Helps communication	Hinders communication
Stating expectations clearly	Giving mixed messages
Focusing on the problem (not the child)	Accusing or blaming the child
Praising and encouraging effort	Cajoling and bribing cooperation
Asking questions and listening	Making assumptions/judgments
Talking and relating observations	Lecturing, demanding, or directing
Giving responsibility and control	Using condescension and babying
Demonstrating trust and respect	Using sarcasm, insults, or threats
Negotiating compromises	Giving in or giving up
Providing choices	Using threats

Adding Cues that Prompt Good Behavior

In addition to avoiding or changing circumstances associated with problem behavior, another useful strategy is for us to add cues that prompt our children to use good behavior. We need to establish clear rules, routines, and boundaries for our children and remind them of expectations. For example, children may need to know what actions are expected at the dinner table, when and how they should invite friends over, and what the boundaries in the neighborhood are (e.g., how far away they are allowed to travel without an adult, whose houses they may visit). In some cases, the only necessary action is to say exactly what the rules are. In other cases (e.g., with a young child, with a confrontational teenager), it may help for us to include written reminders or pictures (e.g., some pictures to indicate where toys should be put away, a chore list on the refrigerator).

It is important that our expectations are reasonable given our children's ages and capabilities and that the expectations are presented in a way our children can easily understand. For example, it may be helpful for us to differentiate between when we are requesting, demanding, or offering a choice. We should use different language when

- Asking children if they would like to do a certain action (e.g., "How about we go to the store?" "Would you like to watch television?")

- Telling children they have to do a certain action (e.g., "I need you to mow the lawn" "Your homework has to be done before 7:00")

- Providing choices (e.g., "Would you like to wash the car or the dog?" "Would you like to clean your room or practice the piano first?")

Many problems can be prevented by simply explaining to our children what events are going to occur and what is expected of them and reviewing those expectations with our children before facing any new situation. This means clearly stating where we are going, who else will be there, how long we will stay, and exactly what we want our children to do and say while we are there. We cannot assume that our children instinctively know how to accomplish what we want them to; we must teach them how to do what is expected. For example, when taking a child to a parent's place of work, the parent might say, "We are going to stop by my office for a few minutes. After I park the car, we will hold hands and walk into the building. When we enter the building, I expect you to use a quiet voice and keep your hands to yourself. If someone comes up to us and says hello, please respond politely by shaking hands and saying hello back. When I am using my computer, you can look at the book we brought or draw on a pad of paper."

Some children have problems when an activity goes on too long or they have to wait for something they want. In these cases, we might remind our children of our expectations by saying something such as, "We're almost done. I think you can stay in your seat and look at a book for 5 more minutes." With very young children or children with special needs, we might use timers or count down (5 more minutes, 4 more minutes, and so forth) to remind our children of when they will be done. In general, the use of cues (subtle prompts to remind children of expected behavior) can prevent many types of problem behavior. Figure 13 illustrates some strategies to prevent problems based on the case examples.

Illustrations of Strategies to Prevent Problem Behaviors		
Deon	**James**	**Brittany**
When problems occur: During the times Adrienne focuses her attention on someone or something other than him During chaotic circumstances or activities with unfamiliar people At times he is hungry, tired, or sick	When problems occur: During extended play or interactions with younger children in less structured situations	When problems occur: After she is asked to participate in physical activities or interact with her peers After she is stopped from doing activities she likes During socially demanding situations or when the situation expectations are unclear
Preventing problems: Provide Deon with comfort or help (e.g., cuddle with him, get him a snack) before beginning an activity requiring undivided attention. Let Deon know when Adrienne needs some time to herself and what she wants him to do while she is busy (e.g., "I need to make a quick call while you are playing," "Please look at the books while I make dinner"). Give Deon special toys or activities when Adrienne's attention is going to be withdrawn for more than a few minutes (e.g., box of toys just to play with only when Adrienne is cooking dinner).	Preventing problems: Monitor James more closely when he plays with Julie and other children so that his parents can intervene before he hurts them. Establish rules for playing with others (e.g., take turns, talk politely to each other) and review them with James's peers and adults who may be supervising them. Interrupt play periodically and have the children play a different game before problems begin (e.g., after 10 or so minutes).	Preventing problems: Develop a schedule of activities so that Brittany knows what is expected of her daily and put it in writing. Give Brittany a clear warning (e.g., a time limit) before asking her to stop reading about or discussing outer space (e.g., "In 5 minutes I'm going to ask you to come to dinner"). Have Brittany keep her books and personal digital assistant (PDA) out of sight when participating in other activities. Describe social situations and expectations clearly before asking Brittany to

(continued)

Figure 13. Illustrations of strategies to prevent problem behaviors for the three example children.

Figure 13. *(continued)*

Illustrations of Strategies to Prevent Problem Behaviors		
Deon	**James**	**Brittany**
Remind Deon to use words (e.g., "help please") or gestures when he needs something.	Encourage Julie and the younger children to walk away from James rather than fight back with him.	take part in them and rehearse the ways she can participate. Ask peers to explain things to Brittany when she seems uncomfortable.

Activity: Preventing Problems

What circumstances seem to prompt your child's problem behavior?

_____

_____

How can you change these things to prevent problems?

Avoid difficult situations:

_____

_____

Make problem situations better:

_____

_____

Add cues to prompt appropriate behavior:

_____

_____

REPLACING BEHAVIORS

Problem behavior—although irritating, disruptive, or even dangerous—should be seen as simply a means to an end and the way in which children communicate their needs. Children misbehave because it currently seems like the best or most effective option they have for dealing with their circumstances or getting the outcomes they want. Therefore, our most important goal when addressing problem behavior is to encourage our children to develop more appropriate ways of behaving that ideally will replace their problem behavior. A question that can guide us in coming up with replacement behavior is, "What else could my child do to get what he or she needs, to avoid or delay a difficult situation, or to deal with particular circumstances more appropriately and effectively?"

Replacement behaviors for children can include the following: communicating their needs more appropriately, cooperating better with others, becoming more independent in daily activities, and tolerating or coping with difficult circumstances. Some examples follow.

- If our children misbehave when they are uncomfortable, we can teach them to take care of their own physical needs (e.g., get a snack when they are hungry, take a rest when they have a headache).

- If our children get frustrated with particular activities (e.g., homework, chores), we can have them take breaks, divide tasks into smaller steps, change activities, or do relaxing exercises periodically.

- If our children have problems with actions someone else is doing, we can encourage them to express themselves verbally, avoid the uncomfortable interaction, or get help (e.g., say, "stop that," walk away, find an adult).

- If our children misbehave in order to get attention, we can teach them a more appropriate way to ask for it (e.g., say, "I want to play now" or "I need to talk to you") or to learn to entertain themselves for a while.

- If our children usually respond inappropriately (e.g., throwing tantrums, fighting) to having preferred items or toys taken away, we can teach them to politely request the item's return, to take turns, or to plan to use the item later.

The biggest difficulty in replacing problem behavior with more appropriate ways of dealing with circumstances is that our children may have been effectively using their problem behavior for some time and may therefore be very comfortable using it. In order to replace problem behavior, the appropriate behavior needs to be just as easy for them to use and work just as well as the behavior of concern (i.e., the payoff has to be as great). For example, children who hit their siblings to get them to stop teasing may find that to be a very efficient and effective strategy (i.e., it stops the teasing right away). If parents require their children to politely explain what is bothering them, that behavior may take longer to work or not work as well. Instead, it may be more effective to have the children simply say "stop" or come and get their parents—at least for the time being. This way the positive behavior will be able to compete with the problem behavior. Figure 14 shows strategies for replacing problem behaviors for Deon, James, and Brittany.

Once we have selected the skills our children need to have (based on the purposes of the children's problem behavior and the circumstances the children are dealing with), we need to teach those skills. For some children, it may be sufficient for parents to describe or show them what they would like them to do. For other children, parents may need to break the skill down and teach the individual steps. For example, Brittany's developmental disability may make it necessary for her to receive additional guidance on appropriate methods of conversation and social interactions.

Strategies for Replacing Problem Behaviors		
Deon	**James**	**Brittany**
Behaviors of concern: Whining, clinging, asking to be picked up	Behaviors of concern: Yelling, refusing to share, teasing, calling others names, hitting, kicking, throwing	Behaviors of concern: Refusing to participate in activities, do chores, or interact with others
Replacing behavior: Encourage Deon to use words (e.g., "Mommy, help up") or to point when he wants something rather than whining. Teach Deon to play by himself for brief periods of time (e.g., demonstrate by using one of his toys while he uses another at the same time, then have him practice using toys or looking at books while doing a short task).	Replacing behavior: Teach James how to get strong emotional reactions from children through other means (e.g., telling jokes). Teach James how to play with other children, share his things, and resolve his problems with words (e.g., "Can you try to do it this way?"). Teach James to relax (e.g., breathe deeply) and walk away when he is angry. Coach James to use these skills with Julie (e.g., as they go outside to play, have James explain how he will handle a disagreement if one comes up).	Replacing behavior: Encourage Brittany to write down and follow her daily schedule, recording which activities she does and which conversations she had (e.g., about what topics, how well she participated, if she enjoyed the activity). Teach Brittany to verbally announce when she is uncomfortable and needs a break (e.g., "I need a little time") or clarification on expectations. Teach her social skills for talking with friends (e.g., ways to start and stop a conversation) and practice the skills until she is comfortable.

Figure 14. Strategies for replacing problem behaviors for the three example children.

Activity: Replacing Behavior

What is your child currently doing that is of concern?

_____

_____

What would you like your child to do instead (i.e., what are possible replacement behaviors)?

_____

_____

_____

_____

The steps or components Brittany might find useful include the following:

1. Make sure the person you want to talk with is not busy doing something else or wait until he or she is free to talk with you.

2. Approach the person and make eye contact; greet him or her by saying, "Hello" or asking him or her something (e.g., "How are you today?").

3. Pick a topic you both might be interested in and introduce that topic (e.g., "What kinds of books do you like to read?").

4. Listen to what the other person has to say and respond; ask questions if you do not understand or if you want more information.

5. When you are finished with the conversation, close it before leaving (e.g., say, "I have to go now. It was nice talking with you").

Encouraging replacement skills in our children require that we communicate our expectations clearly, provide explanations and rationales (why, what, and how) for particular strategies we intend to use, and guide our children to solve their own problems when possible. Further examples and additional resources for this teaching process are provided in the Parenting Resources section in the Bibliography at the end of this book.

MANAGING CONSEQUENCES

Problem behaviors occur because they work—they enable children to get or avoid certain things. What our children get or avoid as a result of their behavior makes them continue that behavior. Knowing the outcomes, results, or consequences of our children's problem behavior helps us to understand what motivates our children and influences changes in their behavior. It also lets us know what is important to our children and what our children are willing to work for (e.g., if children expend a lot of energy by displaying problem behavior in order to avoid an unwanted task or action, imagine what they could accomplish by channeling that energy into positive behavior). Using this understanding, we can plan strategies by answering this question: "How can I respond to my child's behavior so that the outcomes he or she is seeking are more readily available when using positive behavior and less available for problem behavior?" Ultimately, our goal when managing consequences of behavior is to make sure the purpose or function of our children's behavior is achieved through positive behavior rather than problem behavior. Some examples follow.

- If our children misbehave to get attention from other people, we can ask family members and friends to talk to and praise the children when they are behaving nicely (i.e., catch them being good), but to refrain from giving the children attention when they are misbehaving.

- If our children's behavior problems occur to gain access to an activity, toy, or other highly desired item, we can make sure those items are available only following positive behavior (e.g., requiring the children to ask nicely to get the item they want, allowing television time only after homework has been completed) and withheld following problem behavior.

- If our children seem to enjoy the problem behavior for its own sake (i.e., running and screaming feels good), we can find other ways for them to get that same kind of stimulation (e.g., taking the children to a park on a regular basis and letting them behave as actively as they wish).

- If our children use problem behavior to avoid a task or situation they do not like, we can give them breaks or time off when they are behaving appropriately, but still not allow them to avoid those situations otherwise (e.g., earning a day off from chores if they do their chores without complaining all week). Figure 15 provides examples of strategies to manage consequences for the three example children.

We cannot control everything that happens as a result of our children's behavior (e.g., getting attention from other people, receiving stimulation from the behavior), but the outcomes we can control will probably be enough to see improvement. For consequences to be effective, they need to be specific and consistent. We should talk to our children on a regular basis about the appropriate behaviors our children are already doing and the inappropriate behaviors we want them to change. We should make sure to praise our children for specific behaviors. We should also try to respond to our children's behavior as quickly as possible every time it occurs—particularly in the beginning, when we are trying to create new habits.

Strategies for Managing Consequences		
Deon	**James**	**Brittany**
Purposes of behavior: Getting attention or comfort from Adrienne, getting Adrienne to stop her activities and focus on him	Purposes of behavior: Gaining control over others, obtaining his own enjoyment, getting reactions from the younger children	Purposes of behavior: Avoiding activities and interactions with people
Managing consequences: Only respond to Deon's requests when he uses proper words or gestures. If he whines, ignore him until he stops. Send him out of the room if necessary. When Deon is playing quietly by himself, make a point to reward his behavior (e.g., "You've been playing nicely, now let's snuggle a little").	Managing consequences: When James starts teasing, yelling, or calling names, encourage Julie and the other children to walk away and/or get an adult to intervene, rather than give James the reaction he is looking for. Reward James (and Julie) for playing nicely together with special activities of their choice. Continue to use time-outs when James hurts other kids but stop spanking him (further discussion on this topic takes place in the Concerns Regarding Punishment segment of this chapter). Monitor James's play with other children and reward him when he handles problems appropriately.	Managing consequences: Allow Brittany to have time alone to read or spend time on the computer after completing her required activities and chores or when she asks to be excused appropriately. Allow Brittany to discuss a topic of her interest after she engages in a conversation on a different topic. Avoid stopping interactions or withdrawing demands when Brittany engages in inappropriate behavior. Have Brittany record her interactions with peers and adults (e.g., who she talked to, what they said). Allow Brittany to go to the library or to have credit toward purchasing a new book when she meets her goal for interacting and participating each week.

Figure 15.   Strategies for managing consequences for the three example children.

Positive Consequences

Privileges within parental control (e.g., allowance, access to television, special treats) should be made available to children only when they are behaving appropriately. These privileges can and should be withheld otherwise. Establishing a daily or weekly reward system, which is individualized for each child and family, may clarify parents' expectations and help them be more consis-

Expectations for Brittany	S	M	T	W	R	F	S
Got ready on time in the morning	✔		✔	✔		✔	✔
Completed all school work	✔	✔	✔		✔	✔	
Participated in recreational activities	✔		✔		✔	✔	✔
Set the table/helped make dinner	✔	✔	✔	✔		✔	
Ate dinner and socialized with family		✔		✔	✔	✔	
Interacted with friends (bonus)		✔			✔	✔	
Goal: Earns allowance on 4 out of 5 days	$2.00	$2.00	$2.00	$1.50	$2.00	$3.00	$1.00

Figure 16. Example chart for tracking a rewards system for Brittany.

tent in dispensing rewards. Figure 16 shows how Brittany can earn allowance (which she may use to purchase new books or puzzles) each week for meeting specific expectations.

Negative Consequences

In addition to making sure our children get rewards for positive behavior but not for problem behavior, we may find it helpful or even necessary to deal directly with our children's problem behavior as it occurs. Using natural and logical consequences tends to be the most effective and respectful approach.

Natural consequences refer to the results (i.e., things we can simply allow to happen) that automatically occur when our children behave in a certain way. For example, if children break their own toys, they can no longer play with them; if children continually forget to take their lunch with them to school, they can be hungry at lunchtime. Logical consequences mean that the way we respond to our children's behavior is closely tied to their behavior and makes sense given the situations that have happened. Examples of natural and logical consequences include the following.

1. Clean up your own messes: Have children neatly put away the toys and supplies they use and clean up their own spills (e.g., wipe down the counter after preparing a snack).

2. Time wasted is time lost: If children take too long to do what their parents ask, they lose the time set aside for privileges (e.g., "Yes, you've finished your chores, but now it's too late to watch a movie").

3. Being grouchy is a lonely business: If children are being rude or disruptive, they should not be welcome around the other family members until they can behave appropriately (e.g., the child is sent to his or her room until he or she can be polite again).

These approaches can be applied to the case study involving Deon. For example, Adrienne might base how much time she will spend playing one-to-one with Deon on by how long he plays independently (e.g., 5 minutes of play time for every 5 minutes of independence). She may also decide to allow him to remain in the room with her only if he behaves appropriately (e.g., if he whines, he has to go to another room for a short period).

Two common negative consequences to address problem behavior are the use of time-out and restitution. Time-out involves withdrawing rewards, attention, or other positive consequences for a period of time. It does not mean isolating children for lengthy periods of time or placing them in humiliating situations (e.g., locking them in their room, making them stand with their nose touching the wall)—which would be considered misuses of this method. The primary objective of time-out is to remove children from highly enjoyable situations and place them in rather boring situations for a little while. For example, children may be asked to leave the dinner table until they can discuss appropriate topics or go to their rooms for a couple of minutes to consider better ways of resolving disputes with their siblings.

Restitution involves having children repair, replace, or otherwise be accountable for what they have damaged. It can mean losing privileges that are naturally tied to their action or performing some task to make a situation better (e.g., doing extra chores to earn money to pay for something they have broken). In order to use restitution effectively, it is important to make sure that children understand exactly what they did wrong, how they are expected to improve the situation, and that they are capable of repairing their mistake.

Concerns Regarding Punishment

A natural reaction to our children's problem behavior may be for us to use more extreme forms of punishment when they misbehave. This may mean doing harsh things such as slapping or spanking them, withholding meals from them, yelling at them, or enforcing prolonged periods of restriction on them. These types of punishment may get our children's attention and stop their behavior immediately—possibly just due to the shock effect or fear these actions provoke—however, these types of punishment are also likely to have lasting negative side effects.

First, punishment tends to be overused. Because punishment often works so effectively and results in children stopping their problem behavior immediately, it is an enticing choice. In addition, punishment can release some of our own tension, which can be reinforcing. Therefore, using punishment encourages it to be used again. Punishment can easily become a self-perpetuating, vicious cycle.

Second, the effects of punishment are commonly short-lived and situation specific (i.e., it works only when and where we can follow through with it). We could end up feeling like we have to punish our children all of the time or with increasing levels of severity in order to control their behavior. We may find that our children behave worse in public places or other situations where we do not feel comfortable punishing them.

Third, punishment does not teach children about appropriate behavior; rather, it focuses on stopping or suppressing behavior. Children do not learn how to behave via punishment—they simply learn what behaviors (and therefore consequences) should be actively avoided. Because of this, they may be less likely to take initiative and seek new ways to solve problems and instead focus on staying out of trouble, or at least on not getting caught.

Finally, punishment can have emotional side effects. Our children may come to view us in a negative way, retaliate against us, or stop interacting with us, resulting in lasting damage to our parent–child relationships. If we rely on punishment, we are no longer providing positive role models for respectful interaction and self-control. For all these reasons, the use of punishment should be minimized.

Managing Crises

Sometimes children behave in ways that can endanger themselves or other people. In those cases, it may be necessary for us to physically remove our children from a situation (e.g., pick them up and carry them away), block our children's behavior (e.g., stand between them and another child), briefly confine our children (e.g., hold onto them until they calm down), or get another adult's attention and aid (e.g., call for help). This type of crisis management should not be considered a punishment or a solution but a necessary way for us to ensure the safety of the children, families, and property involved until we are able to develop a better plan for managing the behavior. If these methods are required to manage crises, they should be used nonaggressively (i.e., with the least amount of verbal or physical force necessary) and only long enough for us to help our children to regain control of their own behavior. These principles can be applied to the case study involving James. His parents need to intervene quickly when he becomes aggressive toward his sister (e.g., hitting, kicking, throwing things). This might mean that his parents direct him or physically take him to a separate area until he calms down.

Activity: Managing Consequences

What outcomes does your child achieve through his or her behavior?

He or she gets...

_____

_____

_____

He or she avoids...

_____

_____

_____

How will you respond to your child's behavior?

Reward positive behavior (e.g., replacement skills) by...

_____

_____

_____

_____

_____

Deal constructively with problem behavior (e.g., not reward) by...

_____

_____

_____

_____

_____

The strategies we select to prevent problems, replace behavior, and manage consequences should fit together and be integrated as part of a comprehensive plan. It may be helpful for us to keep a record of the strategies we are using (i.e., in a behavior support plan) so that we can refer to it quickly and easily.

SUMMARY

The most important long-term approach for addressing our children's behavior concerns is for us to assist our children in developing more appropriate behaviors in order to meet needs and handle difficult situations. In essence, PBS is about teaching. When we understand the causes and purposes of our children's behavior, we can create a plan to teach our children appropriate ways to behave by preventing problems, encouraging replacement behaviors, and managing consequences.

Before Moving On

 Have you determined what behaviors you will need to address and where and when you plan to address them?

 Using the understanding of patterns you have gained, have you developed strategies to

Prevent problems?

Encourage replacement behavior?

Manage consequences?

CHAPTER 6

Using the Plan

Once we understand the causes and purposes of our children's behavior, identifying strategies and putting them into effect may seem straightforward, but there are a number of issues we should consider to ensure that the strategies we select will work. To effectively implement PBS we must

- Choose strategies that are right for both our children and families.

- Make adjustments to complement broader life issues that may be affecting our children's behavior.

- Arrange for necessary resources, support, and communication before putting the strategies into action.

- Create ways to monitor the changes in behavior and the achievement of broad goals to make sure the strategies are working.

This chapter discusses these four issues in detail and with examples, guiding how to use behavior plans for our children.

MAKING SURE THE PLAN FITS

When considering possible strategies, it may be obvious that we can choose from a variety of options designed to help us deal with our children's behavior. The best strategies, however, are the ones that are right for our children and that fit within our family. When selecting strategies, we should consider our children's strengths, skills, weaknesses, preferences, and needs (e.g., What do our children like or dislike? What are our children's goals? What do our children need to achieve those goals?). We should choose respectful and unobtrusive approaches for dealing with our children's behavior. For example, we would not want to respond to our children's behavior in ways that embarrass them in front of their peers because that could be counterproductive. To make sure our plans fit with the circumstances involved, we should discuss our concerns and ideas with our children—explaining which behaviors are of concern and why, what patterns of behavior we have observed, and how we feel the inappropriate behavior should be addressed—and get our children's input whenever possible.

Whether we carry out our plans depends on our commitment and the degree to which strategies are feasible. We need to believe in and be comfortable with the strategies we are using because if the strategies do not seem right for our particular circumstances, we are less likely to follow the strategies through to a successful behavior change. What actions we take to address our children's behavior should be of reasonable effort and not disrupt typical routines unnecessarily. We should think about the resources available to our families and select strategies that are practical given those resources. Considerations that can affect how well strategies fit may include

- Time: If we are very busy (e.g., work long hours, have many children to care for), time-consuming strategies are not realistic.

- Energy: If we are exhausted, it is hard for us to address our children's behavior consistently (e.g., we might avoid correcting our children's misbehavior because we just want to rest after a long day at work).

- Material resources: If we are purchasing items (e.g., rewards for positive behavior, special tools for implementing the strategies) on a daily or weekly basis, the financial expense can add up.

- Locations: If we need to deal with a problem behavior in many different places, a single strategy or approach for the behavior may not be appropriate (e.g., it may not be reasonable to respond by ignoring a temper tantrum in a public place).

- Coordination: If we can engage and work with other people who care for and interact with our children (e.g., extended family members, teachers, baby sitters, coaches), we may have greater consistency with using their strategies (see Chapter 10 for tips on parents and other adults working together to support positive behavior).

- Family dynamics: If we are thoughtful about the relationships between members of our families, roles that different family members may assume (e.g., disciplinarian, scheduler, playmate), and typical routines and cultural practices of our families, we may find that we can design behavior plans and strategies that work better for everyone. For instance, we would want to consider the impact certain strategies might have on other family members (e.g., if increased attention or privileges for one child would be perceived as unfair) and the degree to which strategies would fit within our daily schedules and cultural traditions.

All of these considerations can affect what strategies seem appropriate and comfortable to use within our families. Before putting our plan into action, we should look back at the strategies identified in Chapter 5 and consider the following questions:

- Do we have enough time to put the strategy in place?

- Do we have enough energy to use the strategy consistently?

- Do we have the resources we need to make the strategy work?

- Does the strategy fit within our families' values and needs?

- Does everyone using the strategy agree with it and agree to use it consistently?

If we determine that some aspect(s) of our plans will not work, adjustments need to be made. For example, in Deon's situation, Adrienne might feel that she cannot ignore his whining when other people are at the house and therefore may decide to redirect him immediately instead. In Brittany's case, allowing her to purchase books as a reward for positive behavior could quickly become far too expensive to maintain, so Nathan may have to put reasonable limits on what she spends.

IMPROVING LIVES

In creating plans to address our children's behavior, we should revisit the broader goals that we wanted to achieve (see Establishing Broader Goals in Chapter 3) and make sure that we are addressing any lifestyle issues that might have an impact on our children's actions (see Analyzing Patterns in Chapter 4). As mentioned previously, when children or adults are generally unhappy or uncomfortable, it affects how they behave on a daily basis. Therefore, we may need to consider and address those circumstances for our children. Some questions we may want to think about are

- Are there any physical or medical conditions that may be affecting our children's behavior (e.g., problems with diet, sleep, allergies)?

- Are our children doing enough pleasurable activities (e.g., visiting places they enjoy, doing events they like), or are our children bored and in need of a change?

- Do our children have enough opportunities to make their own choices and exert some control over their own lives (e.g., able to choose to do homework before dinner or after)?

- Do our children seem content with their typical schedules and daily routines, or are the schedules overcrowded and frustrating (e.g., too many after-school activities)?

- Are our children comfortable in their surroundings (e.g., share a room with noisy or messy siblings)?

- Can we make changes to improve our children's relationships with their friends and family members (e.g., provide a grandparent with tips about our children's preferences)?

These types of broad adjustments to our children's lives will improve their overall behavior and even make using the other strategies less necessary. Figure 17 shows strategies for the children in the three case examples.

Strategies for Improving Lives		
Deon	**James**	**Brittany**
Make sure Deon gets naps, meals/snacks, and medical treatment when needed.	Try to find activities that are of common interest to James, Julie, and the neighborhood children; do those activities with them in an attempt to improve their relationships (e.g., marking off a foursquare court in the driveway, setting up a roller hockey goal and game at the end of the street).	Review Brittany's daily schedule to make sure she has plenty of time to do enjoyable things (e.g., reading) at home, school, and the recreational center.
Plan special time with Deon individually throughout the day (e.g., give him a cuddle, play with him on the floor, talk to him about what he's doing for a few minutes).		Work with Brittany to expand her interests to other topics (maybe topics initially related to outer space—e.g., membership in a science club).

Figure 17.   Strategies for improving the lives of the three example children.

Activity: Improving Lives

What changes can you make in your child's life that might improve his or her behavior?

_____

_____

_____

_____

_____

PUTTING THE PLAN IN PLACE

Once we are satisfied with our plan for dealing with our children's behavior, it is time to put the plan into place. Whereas it is not always necessary to create a formal behavior support plan when intervening in our children's behavior, it is often beneficial to put a plan in writing to be used as future reference. Plans may include goals and behaviors of concern, patterns identified, and specific strategies to be used, as well as action plans and monitoring methods. A blank behavior support plan is included in the Appendix A at the end of this book for frequent photocopying. To make our plan work, we may need support from other people who care for and interact with our children, such as teachers, baby sitters, neighbors, and extended family members. We may need to get organized: rearrange things within our homes, change our schedules, set up a method for recording behavior events and/or outcomes of the plan, and make other necessary preparations to help the plan go smoothly. It is often useful to create an action plan that lists exactly what we need to do in order to put the plan into action. Examples of action plan steps to include follow (see Figure 18 for a sample):

1. Talk to the child about the plan, making sure to explain the behaviors that are expected, ways in which parents and others will help support positive behavior, rewards for appropriate behavior, and consequences for inappropriate behavior.

2. Review the plan with other adults who care for the child and arrange to get support from them.

3. Obtain all necessary materials for initiating the plan.

4. Review the plan regularly to ensure no steps have been forgotten or overlooked.

Brittany's Action Plan

Brittany, Nathan, Margaret, Brittany's teachers, and the recreation supervisor worked together on a person-centered plan for Brittany. Based on the goals identified from the plan and strategies identified based on the information gathering and analysis, Brittany's team has come up with the following plan:

1. Nathan, Margaret, the teachers, and the supervisor at the recreation center will develop a schedule of chores and activities (allowing Brittany to select chores/activities among options).
2. Nathan will help Brittany set up her PDA in a way that allows her to record her daily schedule and participation in conversations and activities. He will teach her to use it for recording purposes and inform her teachers and recreation supervisor of the tool and its purpose.
3. Brittany and Nathan will develop a list of topics for appropriate conversations and practice talking about those topics. Brittany's special education teacher will help her do the same at school.
4. Brittany's special education teacher and recreation supervisor will explain social situations to Brittany and remind her of topics she can discuss and skills she can use to end conversations or activities when she feels uncomfortable. They will also identify and work with peers who can help Brittany in the same way.
5. Brittany and her team members will review other strategies that could fit in her plan, in order to prevent problems and respond to her changing behavior needs, and they will implement these strategies as necessary.

Each Sunday, Brittany and Nathan will review the previous week's events and record the coming week's schedule of activities in her PDA.

Figure 18. Example of an action plan for Brittany.

Activity: Action Plan

Develop a list of steps you must complete in order to implement your plan. Do not forget to explain the plan to your child, communicate with other people, obtain the materials you need, and track the plan and its outcomes.

What needs to be done?	By whom?	When?

Once all action steps have been taken into consideration, it is time to begin using the plan. A plan must be implemented consistently to be effective. This is especially important when first using the plan as our children and ourselves are both learning new patterns of behavior. Being consistent means that we follow through (we do what we say we are going to do) and use the plan as it was designed. As we begin to use the plan, we need to remember that we are accustomed to responding to our children's behavior in particular ways. If we are not careful, we can fall back into those established habits. It may be better to abandon strategies we are finding difficult rather than to implement the plan inconsistently. Therefore, it is important to review the plan periodically and work together with all the people who care for our children to make sure that everyone is using the plan as designed.

Another important consideration is that it can take time for the positive behavior changes to occur. Depending on how ingrained our children's problem behaviors are, the manner in which we have responded to their behavior in the past, and other issues, our children may respond to PBS at different rates. For example, if we have been inconsistent in how we dealt with our children's behavior (e.g., sometimes scolding, sometimes giving in to the behavior or letting it go uncorrected), our children's behaviors are likely to be more established and therefore more resistant to change. We may actually see a brief increase in problems as our children test the newly set limits and try to provoke us into the reactions they are accustomed to getting.

Strategies to prevent problems often have immediate results (i.e., because our children are no longer coming in contact with the situations that precipitated problem behavior). As mentioned before, however, simply preventing problems from occurring is insufficient. In order to produce long-term, durable changes in behavior, we must develop new skills—and that can take time. Given all of this, it is important for us to be patient and do our best to be consistent with the plan. The next segment of this chapter will discuss how we can monitor the results of the behavior changes and make adjustments to the plan when needed.

MONITORING RESULTS

We put a lot of effort into understanding our children's behavior and creating strategies to alter it. Once those strategies have been initiated, however, it is important to make sure the strategies are working and, if they are not, to make any changes as they are needed. Monitoring the results of the plan involves observing how the plan works on a daily basis, deciding if the plan's goals are being achieved, and making adjustments to the plan as needed. It is important for us to be as objective as possible when deciding whether our children's behavior is improving. If we established a starting point at the beginning of the process (i.e., deciding how long, often, or serious a child's behavior was before working to change the behavior), we may simply compare how our children are behaving now to how they were behaving before and note any changes. Monitoring results is most effectively achieved through a collaborative discussion among children and adults involved in the plan. Based on how often problem behaviors occurred before the plan and how often the behaviors are currently occurring, we need to decide how frequently we will review the plan and outcomes (e.g., daily, weekly, monthly). If problem behaviors do not occur very often, we can probably just take note of them when they occur and monitor results in that way. If problems happen frequently or seem to be very complicated, however, it may be beneficial to use a recording system to track progress (e.g., journal, daily rating, tallies). Here are some questions we may ask when evaluating outcomes (Figure 19 offers a sample form for keeping track of this information):

- "Is my child's problem behavior decreasing?"

- "Is my child using his or her replacement behaviors more?"

- "Am I able to consistently use all of the strategies in the plan?"

- "Have there been other positive outcomes for my child and family (e.g., can we go to more places or do more things together?)"

Outcomes of the Plan

Outcomes Date →						
Have the behaviors of concern decreased?	Y N	Y N	Y N	Y N	Y N	Y N
Are other, more positive behaviors being used more often?	Y N	Y N	Y N	Y N	Y N	Y N
Have other positive outcomes occurred? If so, what:	Y N	Y N	Y N	Y N	Y N	Y N
Is everyone in the family happy with the plan and the changes?	Y N	Y N	Y N	Y N	Y N	Y N

Figure 19.   Example form for evaluating outcomes.

By monitoring the results, we have the necessary information for celebrating successes and giving specific feedback to our children on how their behavior is improving. We can also use this information to make adjustments to the plan if it is not working as effectively as hoped or if our families' life circumstances change. For example, we might discover that our plans for our children's behavior work well initially, but then—as our children start visiting more places and interacting with new people—the plans cease to be effective. We would then have to consider those new situations and how to change the plan to make sure it functions within the new circumstances. Figure 20 provides monitoring strategies for the three case examples.

Sample Strategies for Monitoring Results

Deon	James	Brittany
Keep a daily journal that includes all information on the most severe episodes of whining each day, noting when, where, and with whom his whining occurs. Review the results every evening after Deon is asleep.	Rate each day how well James plays with Julie and his peers (3 = *great*, 2 = *okay*, 1 = *lousy*). Review the results every weekend.	Use self-monitoring records in which Brittany lists what activities she does and who she interacts with. Review the results on Sundays with Brittany.

Figure 20.   Sample strategies for monitoring results for the three example children.

☀ Activity: Monitoring Results

What will you do to monitor and evaluate the results of your child's plan?

_____

_____

_____

_____

_____

Through PBS, we can make significant improvements in our children's behavior and lives. Using the case examples, we might look for the outcomes:

• Deon's whining has decreased to no more than once per day, and it lasts for less than 2 minutes when it does occur.

• When James gets frustrated while playing with Julie or younger peers, he walks away before becoming violent.

• Brittany says that she is enjoying being with people and is participating in daily activities with more enthusiasm than ever.

SUMMARY

PBS involves creating plans based on understanding; the plans include strategies to prevent problems by changing the circumstances related to the problem behavior, replacing problem behavior with more positive alternatives, and managing consequences so that our children are encouraged to behave more appropriately. These various strategies must be integrated into a plan that fits well with the personalities and situations of our children and families, and the strategies should be used consistently. The outcomes of the plan (e.g., changes in children's behavior) should be monitored to ensure the plan is working as it was intended.

As children mature and develop new skills and/or their environment changes (e.g., a divorce, a move, a new school, some new friends), additional issues and problems may arise. PBS should be seen as an ongoing process that can be repeated as often as needed. It should also be used in a way that fits comfortably and naturally into the typical routines of our families. These issues are discussed at length in Section IV.

Before Moving On

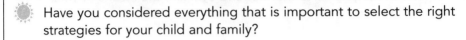 Have you considered everything that is important to select the right strategies for your child and family?

Have you created an action plan for putting the strategies in place?

Have you decided how you are going to monitor the results of your plan?

Stories of Positive Behavior Support

Practicing the Process
Through Case Illustrations

Sections I and II presented the principles and the process of PBS, using the examples of Deon, James, and Brittany to illustrate. The focus of Section III is to share more comprehensive stories of children and their families as they encountered behavioral concerns and addressed them using the PBS process. The detailed, step-by-step experiences of these families will reinforce and expand upon the PBS approach described in previous sections. Each story includes the following:

- A brief background on the child and family, the important issues in their lives, and a short history of the problem

- A description of how the family engaged in the five steps of the PBS process

- A reflection on the PBS process and strategies taken to correct the problem and how well the strategies worked

Each story is unique in terms of the child's age and characteristics, behaviors of concern, family circumstances, factors affecting the child's behavior, and the strategies selected to address the behavior and monitor outcomes. Although there are differences in how each family approached the PBS steps, the principles and basic process remained consistent. It may be apparent from reading these stories that there is a wide variability in the methods that can be used to gather and analyze information and in the different level of details the plans themselves contain. Depending on the problems and circumstances we face, we may apply the PBS process very systematically and carefully (e.g., using the written procedures shown in Section I and II) or very informally (e.g., relying on simply watching, talking, and reflecting on the issues).

Section III provides a chance for us to apply the principles of PBS through the use of models, prompting and guiding us through the process using the stories of Zoë, Isobel, and Michael. Throughout the three stories, *What Do You Think?* activities are inserted to give us an opportunity to consider what actions we might take given the information presented and the particular child and family in the story. After the activities, detailed explanations of the actions taken by the families are provided.

In the first two stories (Zoë and Isobel), the PBS process is necessarily more formal and involved. These stories present detailed examples of the process involving extensive data collection and a wide variety of strategies to address the problem behaviors. The third story (Michael) provides an example of a less involved, but no less effective, approach. This is an example of a situation in which PBS is implemented informally but still produced positive results for the child and family, which is most often the case. This example is included to focus on the central theme of PBS—how understanding behavior and its context leads to the development of positive, creative, and manageable solutions. Concise examples of the children's final behavior support plans are included in Appendix B at the end of this book.

The goal of Section III is to help us become more comfortable with PBS as we go through the illustrations of the process and apply the practices to real-life situations. These stories bring PBS to life and show us how to make it a working tool.

CHAPTER 7

Zoë's Story

Zoë is a 4-year-old girl with a precocious nature. She loves to perform for those around her and spends a lot of time acting out videos, especially when an audience is available. Her parents encourage her to perform and enjoy showing off her talents. She has many friends in her preschool and enjoys her mornings at school and play dates. She tends to be a leader among her friends. Her days are very busy and she no longer takes time to nap. Her mother, Helena, describes Zoë as loving, bubbly, and full of pep. Zoë can also be obstinate and bossy with her friends and her parents.

Zoë's family lives in the suburbs. Helena left her job when she was pregnant with Zoë and, although money is tight, the family seems to be handling it okay. Zoë's father, Alex, works for a television station selling commercial time and commutes in and out of the city by train. Both parents thrive on routine and organization. The entire family enjoys staying busy and is constantly involved in projects or activities. Alex has long hours and usually comes home around 8:00 P.M. Helena and Alex just had a new baby girl, Kora, 6 months ago. Zoë seems to enjoy the idea of having a sister but does not give Kora much attention.

Until recently, Zoë would go to sleep without much difficulty. She would take a bath, get into her pajamas, and brush her teeth at approximately 7:30 each evening. Helena would put Zoë in bed and either parent would lie down and read to her. One of the parents would then dim the lights, give Zoë her teddy bear, rub her back, and leave the room. Zoë would usually have a restful night, waking only periodically when ill or awakened by unusual noises. In the morning, she would wake up perky and ready for the new day.

Now Zoë resists going to sleep. The difficulty begins at bath time, when Zoë disrobes and begins running around the house. Helena tries to joke with her and coax her to the tub but ultimately becomes angry and has to make her take a bath. Zoë gets out of the tub easily and puts on her pajamas. After one of Zoë's parents reads three books of Zoë's choice and rubs her back for 5 minutes (a routine which had been previously established), Zoë refuses to stay in her bed. The other parent, who had been caring for Kora, usually comes in at this point to say goodnight to Zoë. After both parents say good night, Zoë starts to whine and sit up in bed. Her parents leave the room, telling Zoë that it is time to go to sleep. Zoë insists that the light be left on. When her parents go downstairs, Zoë repeatedly calls for them from her room and then proceeds to come down to the family room where her parents are watching television or reading the newspaper, either alone or with Kora. Helena usually walks Zoë back to her room.

Zoë starts to cry when Helena leaves the room again. This pattern happens at least two more times. After taking Zoë back to her room and trying the tactics of negotiating, bribing, yelling, threatening, and eventually screaming, Helena is exhausted and often lies down and subsequently falls asleep in Zoë's bed. She eventually slips out of Zoë's room and goes back to her own room. Zoë awakens during the night, calls for Helena, and then goes to her parents' bedroom. Alex usually walks Zoë back to her bed at this point. He has tried numerous plans, such as locking Zoë in her room and returning to his own room, but this causes Zoë to really get out of control. She kicks the walls, breaks her toys, pounds on the door, and stays up crying for as long as 2 hours. Alex has also tried putting up a gate at Zoë's bedroom door, but she climbs over it the minute he leaves her room and runs back into her parents' room. Both parents are worried that Zoë will hurt herself either by climbing over the gate or by banging into a sharp edge of a broken toy or piece of furniture during a tantrum. Her parents have even resorted to locking their own bedroom door, but after pounding on their door for 30 minutes, Zoë will get a butter knife from the kitchen drawer and try to break open the lock on their door.

Both parents have been inconsistent in dealing with Zoë's nighttime behavior. Sometimes they calmly discuss the issue with Zoë and other times they yell at her immediately (often depending on how they are feeling). Sometimes Alex gets so frustrated that he thinks spanking might be the answer to changing Zoë's problem behavior. Her parents are both exhausted, and caring for a new baby only makes it harder to be patient with Zoë. They feel that Zoë's behavior is disrupting the entire family and damaging their relationships with both of their daughters and with each other. Given the circumstances, they have decided to try to look at Zoë's behavior more closely so that they can be more consistent and effective in dealing with it.

STEP 1: ESTABLISHING GOALS

The first step in PBS is for us to identify goals, define and prioritize specific behaviors of concern, and establish larger, lifestyle goals for our children and families.

Defining the Problem Behavior(s)

Behaviors of concern must be defined clearly. We should make the definitions as specific as necessary to ensure that the behaviors would be identifiable to people who have even casual interactions with our children. We also want to estimate the frequency (how often), duration (how long), and seriousness (how intense) of the behaviors at the outset, so we will be able to assess the change later. Remember, behavior is anything a person says or does.

What Do You Think?

Given what is going on with Zoë and her family, what would you identify as her primary behavior(s) of concern?

Behavior(s): _____

_____

_____

Description: _____

_____

_____

Frequency, duration, and seriousness: _____

_____

_____

Zoë's parents realized that although Zoë has been stubborn in the past, it has not affected her bedtime and sleeping until recently. They wanted to get Zoë to 1) go to sleep and 2) stay in bed all night, and they see both of those actions as one main behavior problem.

Behavior: Leaving her bedroom and being disruptive at bedtime.

Description: Whining, crying, calling for her parents, sitting up or getting out of bed, and leaving her bedroom. These behaviors sometimes escalate to kicking walls, throwing toys, screaming, and flailing her body.

Frequency, duration, and seriousness: This goes on for at least an hour each night and makes it impossible for the family to get enough sleep.

Determining If the Behavior Is Really a Problem

Part of identifying goals is for us to decide whether the behaviors of concern are severe enough to warrant addressing them. Consider the Big Ds. Are the behaviors dangerous, destructive, disruptive, disgusting, or developmentally inappropriate?

What Do You Think?

Look at the definition of Zoë's behaviors of concern and decide whether her behavior is really a problem according to the ideas behind the Big Ds.

Dangerous: _____

_____

Destructive: _____

_____

Disruptive: _____

_____

Disgusting: _____

_____

Developmentally inappropriate: _____

_____

Zoë's parents considered the Big Ds and decided that her behavior was definitely worthy of their attention for the reasons shown in Table 3. Zoë's parents did not consider her behaviors to be disgusting, but they were not sure if they should consider them developmentally inappropriate. They decided to talk with Zoë's pediatrician about it. The pediatrician told them that it is common for preschool-age children to have sleeping difficulties because new fears (e.g., fear of the dark, fear of abandonment) begin to emerge at this time. Also, the feeling of being displaced by a new sibling can create the need for extra attention from parents and reassurance of connection. Sleep issues, the pediatrician stressed, do not, however, have to undermine bedtime or create a dangerous and disruptive environment.

Establishing Broad Goals

In addition to defining behaviors of concern, we also want to consider what broader goals we want to achieve for our children and families. Broad goals

Table 3. Zoë's Big Ds for leaving the bedroom and being disruptive at bedtime

Dangerous	Zoë could get hurt when wandering around the house in the dark. Some nights her behavior escalates to throwing toys and trying to pry open a locked door, which could result in her being injured.
Destructive	Throwing things and prying locks can cause damage.
Disruptive	Zoë's nighttime antics keep everyone awake. Fatigue and frustration is damaging to family morale.
Disgusting	No.
Developmentally Inappropriate	Do not know. Her parents thought that by the age of 4 Zoë should be able to stay in bed by herself.

go beyond just stopping a problem behavior into things like improving relationships, building opportunities, and maintaining emotional well-being.

What Do You Think?

What broad goals might you identify for Zoë and her family?

_____

_____

_____

_____

_____

Zoë's parents considered both Zoë's needs and their own needs and decided on these goals:

- Zoë will fall asleep independently, remaining in her own room through the entire night (and feel safe and content).
- Bedtime will be a happy, peaceful period for the whole family.
- The family will be rested, relaxed, and generally comfortable with one another.

Zoë's parents realized that having a peaceful, independent bedtime was their goal and not Zoë's. Zoë would prefer to be with her parents and receive the reassurance that she gets from their presence (especially since Kora has come along).

STEP 2: GATHERING INFORMATION

The second step in PBS is for us to gather information to better understand our children's behavior. Many parents find they can easily get this information by watching their children in different situations (e.g., where and with whom does the behavior take place), talking to others (e.g., teachers, doctors, other parents) who interact with their children, and recording their children's behavior (e.g., by writing in a journal, by marking on a chart).

Decide What Information to Collect

We must select methods for gathering the types of information that will be helpful to us and determine the best way to use those methods.

What Do You Think?

What methods of information gathering might Zoë's parents use?

Watching: _____

_____

_____

Talking: _____

_____

_____

Recording: _____

_____

_____

Once Zoë's parents decided what they wanted to change, they stepped back from operating in crisis mode, and they thought carefully about how to work on understanding Zoë's behavior and what methods they should use to gather the necessary information. Zoë's parents wanted to pick strategies that they would fit into their schedules and that would work well with their capabilities. They decided to do the following

Watching   When Zoë's parents were both home in the evening, they took turns paying attention to Zoë's behaviors and their own reactions to her behaviors, especially at bedtime.

Talking   Helena talked to Zoë about bedtime issues during the day while Kora was sleeping. Zoë's parents got a baby sitter to watch the girls on a Saturday afternoon so they could spend some time together discussing their concerns. They also took time each morning before waking up the children to talk to each other about what had happened the evening before. Given that Zoë's sleep problems were only affecting their family, they did not feel the need to consult with her preschool teachers or extended family members.

Recording   Zoë's parents used a behavior log to record what took place before and after Zoë went to bed each night. They included changes in the bedtime routine, what time they put her to bed, when she went to sleep, what her actions were, how they reacted to her actions, if and when she got up during the night, and any other information that might help them understand her behavior.

Using this plan, Zoë's parents gathered information for approximately 2 weeks, which seemed like a very long time to them. This is what they learned.

Helena sat down alone with Zoë and told her that bedtime was not a happy time for any of the family members and that her behavior was affecting everyone. Zoë shared that she did not like to be alone in her room, she was not tired at bedtime, and she missed her parents because she could hear them having fun with Kora. Helena asked Zoë why she had a problem now, when she used to go to sleep alone, and Zoë said she wanted to be with the family and not be alone.

The behavior log revealed some interesting patterns. The entry shown in Figure 21 is typical of what happened almost every night. Sometimes, however, the ending was different. Every once in awhile, Zoë's parents would spank her and she would stay in bed and fall asleep crying. On two occasions, Zoë's parents locked themselves in their bedroom and Zoë banged on their door until she fell asleep on the floor outside of their room.

Zoë's parents talked with each other about how the bedtime routine has been throughout Zoë's short life. They realized that bedtime used to involve both of them and that they often used to spend extra time with her in the evenings. Since Kora's birth, usually only one parent was involved in the bedtime routine, and because there seemed to be more responsibilities, that parent did not spend as much time putting Zoë to bed as he or she used to. Both parents realized they were beginning to have negative feelings about Zoë because of her nighttime behavior and they seemed to be changing how they interacted with her, especially as nighttime approached. Zoë's parents also realized they were being inconsistent with their reactions to Zoë's behavior. Their reactions

BEHAVIOR LOG		
Name: Zoë Date: June 14		
Situation: Zoë's behavior at bedtime		
What happened before	What Zoë did	What happened after
The bedtime routine ends with Zoë in her bed; we said goodnight, left the room, and went back downstairs.	Zoë whined and jumped on her bed.	We shouted a reminder that it is bedtime and that she should stop and go to sleep.
We gave Zoë a first reminder.	Zoë got out of bed and stood in room calling, whining, and crying.	We shouted another reminder that she should go to sleep, more firmly this time.
We gave Zoë a second reminder.	Zoë left the room and came downstairs, crying and whining.	Helena angrily walked Zoë back to her room, put her in bed, and told her to stay there and go to sleep.
Helena left Zoë's room.	Zoë came downstairs again, crying harder.	Alex walked her back, put her in bed, and locked the door.
Alex left Zoë's room.	Zoë kicked walls, threw toys, and punched the door.	Helena lay down in bed with Zoë, intending to stay and cuddle until Zoë calmed down; they both fell asleep.

Figure 21.   Behavior log showing the actions and reactions of Zoë's family.

ranged from spanking and forcing her to stay in bed to cuddling and sleeping with her.

STEP 3: ANALYZING PATTERNS

The third step in the PBS process is for us to summarize what we know. That means we use the information we collected to identify patterns in the problem behavior and the circumstances surrounding it. We can summarize by writing a sentence or short paragraph that describes the patterns in our children's behavior.

What Do You Think?

Based on the information Zoë's parents collected, what patterns do you feel are affecting her behavior?

When _____

occurs, Zoë does _____

to get/avoid _____.

Zoë's parents considered their conversations, looked over the information they recorded and made some conclusions about her behavior. Zoë's problems at nighttime seemed most likely to be because every other family member stayed awake after she was put to bed, and they were especially likely to occur if her parents were playing with Kora. Zoë's behavior was less difficult if she went to bed after Kora was already asleep, when her parents lay down and snuggled with her until she was asleep, or when she was allowed to sleep in her parents' room. Zoë's problem behavior got her attention from her parents and allowed her to avoid going to sleep by herself. Zoë's parents developed a summary:

"When Zoë is put to bed to go to sleep by herself, she cries, whines, gets out of bed, and becomes destructive and disruptive to get us to stay with her and avoid staying in bed by herself. Her sleep problems have emerged since the birth of Kora, when Zoë was first forced to share our attention."

Zoë's parents were aware that Zoë did not want to go to bed by herself. They were not sure if it was just because she wanted their attention or if she was really having fears and negative feelings or thoughts when she was by herself. Regardless, they felt that the summary accurately described the patterns. They also acknowledged that broader issues were coming into play. Zoë was not having problems with bedtime until Kora arrived. Now her parents were giving her less attention overall.

Testing Guesses

When we are not sure about our summary statements, we may want to test them out by changing the circumstances or outcomes surrounding the problem behavior to see if the behavior still happens—or happens as much.

In Zoë's case, her parents did not feel this was necessary.

STEP 4: DEVELOPING A PLAN

The fourth step in PBS is for us to use the understanding gained in Steps 2 and 3 to create a plan for dealing with our children's behavior.

What, Where, and When to Intervene

Prior to deciding exactly how to address our children's behavior, we need to consider what behaviors we feel we need to address right now and when and where we are going to intervene.

What Do You Think?

What behaviors should Zoë's family address in the plan (e.g., specific behaviors, general ones)?

_____

_____

When should Zoë's parents address problems (e.g., all day, certain times)?

_____

_____

Where should they focus (e.g., at home, at school, in the community)?

_____

_____

It was obvious to Zoë's parents that bedtime was their primary concern. In order to address Zoë's need for attention, however, they also need to look at other times of the day as well. They realized that changing her behavior meant changing their own behavior. It would take time and patience, and they were going to have to choose their battles.

How to Intervene

Comprehensive plans for dealing with our children's behavior include a variety of strategies, including steps to prevent problems, replace problem behaviors with more appropriate behaviors, and manage the consequences of the behavior.

Preventing Problems

Once parents understand what provokes their children's behavior, they can change circumstances (e.g., avoid things that trigger problems) to help their children behave more appropriately.

What Do You Think?

What circumstances prompt Zoë's behavior? _____

_____

_____

How can her parents change the environment to prevent problems?

Avoid difficult situations: _____

_____

_____

Make problem situations better: _____

_____

_____

Add cues to prompt appropriate behavior: _____

_____

_____

Once Zoë's parents had an understanding of the causes and purposes of Zoë's problem bedtime behavior, they felt confident to make changes (including changes in how they were interacting with her) to encourage Zoë to use more appropriate bedtime behavior. Zoë's parents felt that the manner in which they put Zoë to bed was affecting her problem behavior. Specifically, they felt they needed to focus on what behavior they expected of Zoë and how the family nighttime routine was contributing to Zoë's problem behavior at bedtime. Zoë's parents needed to know what activities and influences were causing Zoë to resist going to sleep and what changes they could make in the bedtime routine that would encourage her to stop resisting going to bed. After reviewing the information and patterns, Zoë's parents saw that the following strategies might prevent or minimize problems:

- Spend more quality time with Zoë earlier in the evening. When both parents are home, one can take care of Kora while the other plays with Zoë for 15–30 minutes. If both parents are not home, Helena will put Kora in the baby carrier or swing and go for a walk or dance to videos with Zoë.

- Give Zoë her bath a little earlier in the day so there is more time between the bath and bedtime. Because Zoë associates bathing with being put to bed, an action that has become negative, separating the two activities may keep Zoë from becoming upset prior to bed.

- Make the house quiet when Zoë is going to sleep, because Zoë said that she could hear her parents having fun with Kora in the den. Also, allow Zoë to listen to soft music in bed by using a tape player with an automatic shut-off to drown out the sounds of the house.

- Allow Zoë to pick out a favorite picture to put beside her bed and look at as she is listening to her soft music and getting sleepy to provide comfort and distraction.

- Delay Zoë's bedtime 30 minutes so that Alex can be home to either have special time with Zoë while Helena is with Kora or be with Kora while Helena is with Zoë.

- Remain in the bedroom, sitting away from Zoë in the rocking chair for a couple minutes before leaving the room. Allow Zoë to select a stuffed animal of her choice to serve as a bedtime buddy while she is away from her parents.

- Establish new expectations for the bedtime routine. Helena will read two books to Zoë, rub Zoë's back, and sit in the rocker for 5 minutes, reading her own adult book. She will leave and assure Zoë that she will return to check on Zoë if Zoë remains in bed and quiet. Tell her what the numbers will read on her digital clock in 5 minutes if she chooses to watch the time.

- Return after 10 minutes. Increase the time before checking on Zoë by 5 minutes each week until Helena is only checking on Zoë as she prepares to go to bed herself.

Replacing Behaviors

In addition to preventing problems, we can—and should—teach our children the skills to communicate their needs and cope with difficult situations in appropriate and positive ways.

What Do You Think?

What is Zoë currently doing that is of concern?

_____

_____

_____

What would her parents like her to do instead?

_____

_____

_____

Zoë's parents thought about what Zoë was doing and why, and they reiterated their concerns about her behavior—that she was getting out of bed, crying, whining, coming out of her room, jumping, and throwing things. They determined the behaviors they wanted Zoë to do instead were as follows:

- Stay in bed after her parents leave the room. Remain quiet until she falls asleep. If she wakes up in the middle of the night, calm and comfort herself back to sleep.

- Use the new skills for calming and comforting herself by playing music on the tape player, looking at books, looking at the picture beside her bed, singing quietly to herself, playing mental games (e.g., counting the people who love her, thinking about enjoyable things she did during the day), or using other relaxation techniques.

Managing Consequences

In order for us to replace problem behavior with more positive ways of behaving, we need to manage the outcomes of our children's behavior so that our children are rewarded for positive behavior and not problem behavior.

What Do You Think?

What outcomes does Zoë achieve through her behavior?

She gets...

_____

_____

She avoids...

_____

_____

How should Zoë's parents respond to her behavior?

Reward positive behavior by...

_____

_____

_____

Deal constructively with problem behavior by...

_____

_____

_____

Zoë's parents thought carefully about the purpose of Zoë's disruptive behavior at bedtime and recognized that their inconsistent reactions to her behavior was aggravating the problem. They noticed that by yelling at her and walking back to her bedroom they were giving her the extra attention she wanted, even though the attention was negative. Zoë worked very hard to avoid being alone in her bedroom while her parents were with the new baby. Sleeping with one of her parents next to her was the exact goal Zoë wanted to achieve.

Given this understanding, Zoë's parents decided to respond to her behavior in the following ways in order to reward positive behavior:

- If Zoë stays in her bed without whining or crying, go to her bedroom after approximately 10 minutes for one more snuggle. Each night wait a little longer to go to her. If she stays in her bed and quiet for the entire night, do an activity of Zoë's choice with her the next day while Kora is napping.

- Create a chart to track the successful bedtime experiences and place it in Zoë's room. If Zoë has shown positive behavior (i.e., remains in her bed without whining or crying) the night before, each morning she can put a star on the chart.

- If Zoë uses positive bedtime behavior for a whole week, make arrangements for a baby sitter to watch Kora and take Zoë out for a couple of hours. Treat her to the purchase of a bedtime-related item of her choice (e.g., a night-light, some glow-in-the-dark stars, a stuffed animal, a pair of pajamas, some new music) while out.

Zoë's parents also decided to respond to problem behavior in the following ways:

- If Zoë comes out of her room after being put to bed, walk her back to bed with minimal interaction (e.g., no eye contact or talking) and remind her one time that she can earn an activity for the next day if she stays quietly in her bed.

- If Zoë comes out of her room after one reminder, walk her to bed and close her bedroom door. Explain to Zoë that they will open the door if she remains quiet and in her bed. After 10 minutes, open the door and tell her that they will see her in the morning. If the door has to be shut, Zoë will not get to do the special activity in the morning.

- If Zoë cries or yells, ignore her. If she does something dangerous (e.g., throwing toys), stop her, remove the item from the room, and exit quickly.

Zoë's parents realized that they had been so inconsistent with how they responded to Zoë's problem behavior that it would take some time for Zoë to adjust to their new responses and trust their responses to be reliable. They decided that they would need to support and reassure each other through this difficult adjustment time, but they were certain if they remained consistent in their responses, Zoë's behavior would eventually improve.

Improving Lives

In creating plans to address our children's behavior, we should periodically revisit the broader goals we were hoping to achieve and make sure we are addressing any lifestyle issues that may be having an impact on our children's actions.

What Do You Think?

What changes can be made in Zoë's life that might improve her behavior?

_____

_____

_____

_____

_____

Zoë's parents made plans to enroll Zoë in a "Mommy and Me" class at the local YMCA. They thought that this activity would be a good outlet for Zoë's performance tendencies and provide her with an interest that was specifically hers (something that Kora cannot do) and about which she could feel proud and special.

Putting the Plan in Place

Once we have created a plan to support positive behavior in our children, we need to consider how we are going to initiate and maintain the plan. We should talk with our children and other adults involved in our children's care, obtain any materials we may need, think of ways we can periodically review how well the plan is doing, and adjust or alter the plan if needed.

What Do You Think?

What steps need to be taken to put Zoë's plan into action (and who might be responsible for maintaining that plan)?

_____

_____

_____

_____

_____

Zoë's parents knew it was critical that they be consistent in using the plan every single night. In order to do so, they needed to prepare exactly what they were going to do and say ahead of time. They also needed to get all extra materials ready in advance so they would not have to worry about misplacing or running out of the materials. They did the following things to initiate the plan:

1. During his lunch break at work, Alex purchased a tape player with an automatic shut-off and borrowed relaxation tapes and manuals from the library (so that he and Helena could get other ideas to help Zoë calm herself). He placed a clock in Zoë's room that she could use to watch for the check-in times.

2. Zoë's parents sat down with Zoë and told her about the new bedtime routine and the plan for encouraging her bedtime behavior. They had Zoë practice going to bed and using some relaxation techniques they learned (including some from a book checked out from the public library) during the day when Kora was sleeping.

3. Zoë and Helena worked together to create the bedtime chart and find the stars that would go on it. Helena asked Zoë to think of activities or items that she wanted to earn, and they put pictures of them on the bottom of the bedtime chart.

4. Zoë and Helena looked through their photo albums and favorite magazines to find a picture that Zoë would like to have next to her bed at night.

5. Both parents reviewed the plan and established a schedule for talking about how the plan was going.

STEP 5: MONITORING RESULTS

By regularly monitoring how our children are responding to the plans in place, we can quickly address any problems that might arise and make necessary changes. Monitoring results involves tracking the replacement behaviors as well as the problem behaviors, supervising how well the plan is working, and noting all positive outcomes (even unplanned ones).

What Do You Think?

What should Zoë's parents do to monitor the results of their plan?

_____

_____

_____

_____

_____

During the first week, Zoë's parents spent a few minutes each morning discussing how bedtime went the night before. They reviewed the behavior chart as they talked to verify how Zoë's behavior changed over time. They also considered how consistent they were in using the plan. This discussion gave them an opportunity to address problems as they arose and make modifications in the plan immediately. After the first week, because bedtime was beginning to go more smoothly, they decided to set aside time weekly on Sunday mornings for this discussion.

OUTCOMES FOR ZOË

Preparing for and talking about their new plan went very well for Zoë and her family. Zoë was excited about putting stars on the bedtime chart, using her new tape recorder, and watching the clock in her room. She enjoyed looking through photo albums and magazines and finding special pictures. She seemed to understand the new bedtime procedures, including the differences between what would happen if she followed them and what would happen if she did not.

Even with all of the preparation, however, the family ran into some problems putting the plan in place. Zoë had trouble remembering the check-in time. Her parents calmly and quickly repeated their explanations before they left the room. Although Zoë called out a few times, she managed to stay in bed until she went to sleep the first night, apparently fascinated with the new clock and picture.

On the next few nights, Zoë seemed to be testing the new routine and pushed her parents' limits. When she tried to leave her room, they met her in the hall and ushered her right back to bed. At times, her parents found it difficult to follow the plan. Ignoring Zoë's yelling and crying was hard, but they reassured each other that they were doing the right thing. By the fourth night Zoë seemed to be getting into the routine and finally earned the morning activity.

For the next few weeks Zoë generally did well. Helena, however, was finding it harder to consistently set aside enough time to have special activities with Zoë. She mentioned this to a neighbor who suggested that her 12-year-old daughter, Sarah, might be able to help a few days per week because it was summer and Sarah was generally home. Because Zoë liked Sarah a great deal, Zoë's parents gave her the choice on those days of either doing an activity with Sarah or letting Sarah watch Kora while Helena spent time with Zoë.

Zoë's parents continued to use the plan and make small changes when necessary (e.g., changing the pictures, purchasing new nighttime related items, shifting the schedule when Alex's schedule changed). As time passed and Zoë matured, they found that she no longer remembered to put stars on the bedtime chart and they decided to stop using it. Eventually, bedtime problems were no longer an issue. Zoë and her parents were finally getting enough rest, and they were all happier together.

CHAPTER 8

Isobel's Story

Isobel is a 15-year-old girl with many friends. She is on the telephone or computer every free moment of the day. She is essentially a typical adolescent—prone to giggling with friends over inside jokes one minute, brooding over a boy the next. Isobel is quite concerned about her image with her peers. She is described by the people who know her best as outgoing, flirtatious, opinionated, and (sometimes) argumentative.

Isobel comes from an upper–middle-class family. Her mother, Simone, is an artist and her father, Luis, is a professor at the local university. Isobel has an 11-year-old sister, Maria, and a 9-year-old brother, Aarón. Maria is quiet, respectful, and reserved. She and Isobel are both good students, although Maria has to work harder than Isobel to achieve her scholastic goals. Aarón is the high scorer for his soccer team. Their parents' weekends are consumed with traveling to Aarón's soccer games and watching him play.

Isobel attends a local private school. She attends regularly and makes good grades, but her teachers feel that she has a tendency to push the limits of authority. She questions the school's rules and periodically violates the school's dress code but has not been disciplined severely at school. Isobel participates in drama activities at school, but that involvement is starting to wane. She used to be involved in other activities, such as student council membership and after-school functions, but her participation has begun to diminish in favor of other interests.

Although Isobel is generally respectful with most adults, this is not the case when she interacts with her parents. Each of her parents view her behavior differently. Simone describes Isobel as spirited and often makes excuses for her behavior. Luis uses stronger language, referring to her as rude, nasty, and rebellious. At home, Isobel has vocal outbursts when she does not get her way and whenever her parents ask her to do something that she does not want to do. Even the smallest request can trigger Isobel's problem behavior, sending her storming into her room or out of the house. Luis is very worried that as time goes on, Isobel's negative behavior will get worse and he and Simone will not have any control over her. Isobel insults her parents and criticizes them harshly every chance she gets. Her behavior is affecting the morale of the entire family.

Mealtimes are especially difficult. Simone will call Isobel to come for dinner when it is ready. At that time, Isobel is usually in her room doing homework or listening to (very loud) music, and she rarely responds. After approximately 5 minutes, Simone will call to her again, with still no response from Isobel. Then Simone either calls Isobel very loudly or stands outside her room and makes a direct request for her to come to dinner. At this point, Isobel usually screams at

Simone, admonishing her (e.g., "Can't you see I was doing something?") or becomes sarcastic (e.g., "I guess you are ready for dinner"). Isobel then storms down the stairs to the table. She sits down, pouting and slamming her chair or utensils, and begins to verbally abuse Maria. She typically criticizes the dinner and refuses to eat. Isobel rarely makes eye contact with the rest of the family or speaks other than to snap at her family members. When she does participate in a conversation, it is to respond to direct questions in a sassy and sarcastic way (e.g., complaining that her parents "ask such stupid questions"). Even though the meal has barely begun, Isobel asks if she can leave the table. Isobel says she does not understand why she has to sit at the dinner table if she is not eating. Between the sarcasm and criticism, Isobel disrupts the dinnertime nearly every night.

Isobel also misses her curfew regularly, usually by 20 minutes or more, when she goes out with her friends, and she does not telephone her parents to let them know when to expect her. Luis feels that she pushes the authoritative boundaries to the breaking point. When her parents address the issue of missing curfew with her and tell her how they were worried when they did not know where she was, Isobel dismisses their concerns and complains that they are always making a big deal about nothing. She says things like, "What's the big deal? It's only 10:30, and it's Saturday." When Isobel's parents explain that the problem is not that the hour is late but that she missed her 10:00 curfew by nearly 30 minutes, Isobel tells them she hates them and cannot wait to get out of the house so they would not be able to nag her all the time. Isobel often refuses to answer her parents' questions about where she was, what she was doing, and whom she was with while she was out. Because of Isobel's erratic behavior, her parents suspect that she may be dabbling with alcohol or drugs, but they have no real evidence.

Isobel leaves her room and the rest of the house in a mess. It is impossible to walk through her room without stepping on articles of clothing, piles of schoolwork, and discarded shoes. The space on top of her dresser is piled high with papers, clothes, and other items. She leaves her shoes, clothes, books, and personal items all around the house. When Isobel's parents ask her to pick up these items, Isobel usually ignores her parents' first request or tells them she will clean up later (which she never does). Additional requests often lead to Isobel's making sarcastic comments, responding rudely to her parents, and making verbal outbursts such as screaming and yelling. When pressed, Isobel usually leaves the area by either going to her room or leaving the house, slamming the door behind her as she goes. Her parents threaten that they will throw out the personal items she leaves around or not purchase any new clothes or shoes for her, but they never follow through with the threats.

Isobel's parents respond inconsistently to her, probably in part due to their different views on her behavior. They either try to talk to her about her feelings, explaining why she should be nicer, or they threaten and reprimand her. Simone frequently covers for Isobel's negative behavior by making excuses for why Isobel is acting so negatively (e.g., perhaps she is tired, had a bad day, or had an argument with her friends). Sometimes her parents try to give her unconditional attention and support (e.g., "love her out of it") and other times they ground her. When Isobel is grounded, she is not supposed to go to the mall with her friends, use the computer, talk on the telephone, or watch television. Isobel, however, often does these things anyway. Her parents' consequences do not seem to affect her negative behavior. Only Isobel's immediate family seems to view Isobel's behavior as defiant, perhaps because the behavior is focused on testing the boundaries of parental authority. Her parents are exhausted from interacting carefully with Isobel in hopes to avoid provoking her outbursts.

STEP 1: ESTABLISHING GOALS

The first step in PBS is for us to identify goals, define and prioritize specific behaviors of concern, and establish larger, lifestyle goals for our children and families.

Defining the Problem Behavior(s)

Behaviors of concern must be defined clearly. We should make the definitions as specific as necessary to ensure that the behaviors would be identifiable to people who have even casual interactions with our children. We also want to estimate the frequency (how often), duration (how long), and seriousness (how intense) of the behaviors at the outset, so we will be able to assess the change later. Remember, behavior is anything a person says or does.

What Do You Think?

Given what is going on with Isobel and her family, what would you identify as her primary behavior(s) of concern?

Behavior(s): _____

_____

_____

Description: _____

_____

_____

Frequency, duration, and seriousness: _____

_____

_____

Isobel's parents realized there were two main behaviors that concerned them, which they chose to label as defiance and disrespect. They often saw both behaviors at the same time, but not always. Both behaviors related to how Isobel interacted with her parents specifically.

Behavior: Defiance.

Description: Ignoring instructions, continuing activities after she is told to stop, breaking established house rules and curfew, and leaving the house without permission.

Behavior: Disrespect.

Description: Talking rudely, arguing, screaming, and using sarcasm, insults, and criticism.

Frequency, duration, and seriousness: Both of these behaviors occur a minimum of three times per day and more frequently on weekends. They last until Isobel leaves the room, and they disrupt the entire family.

Determining if the Behavior Is Really a Problem

Part of identifying goals is for us to decide whether the behaviors of concern are severe enough to warrant addressing them. Consider the Big Ds. Are the behaviors dangerous, destructive, disruptive, disgusting, or developmentally inappropriate?

What Do You Think?

Look at the definition of Isobel's behaviors of concern and decide whether her behavior is really a problem according to the ideas behind the Big Ds.

Dangerous: _____

_____

Destructive: _____

_____

Disruptive: _____

_____

Disgusting: _____

_____

Developmentally inappropriate: _____

_____

Isobel's parents considered the Big Ds and decided that her behavior was definitely worthy of their attention for the reasons shown in Table 4. Isobel's parents did not consider her behaviors to be disgusting or destructive. They also did not consider her behaviors to be developmentally inappropriate, because they had heard that this type of behavior is not uncommon for teenagers. After they spoke with Isobel's teachers and other parents of their acquaintance, they found that testing household rules and disregarding authority figures were common actions for young people at Isobel's age but that Isobel's actions seemed to be extreme.

Establishing Broad Goals

In addition to defining behaviors of concern, we also want to consider what broader goals we want to achieve for our children and families. Broad goals go beyond just stopping a problem behavior and include things like improving relationships, building opportunities, and maintaining emotional well-being.

Table 4.   Isobel's Big Ds for Defiance and Disrespect

	Defiance	Disrespect
Dangerous	Isobel refuses to follow rules, especially those related to curfew and to places she may visit, which may put her health and safety at risk.	Isobel argues, yells, and responds rudely in other ways; disrespectful talk is not dangerous.
Disruptive	Isobel refuses to follow directions, which makes it difficult to maintain established rules and routines and sets a bad example for the other children in the house.	Isobel's arguing and yelling disrupt mealtimes and the overall harmony of the home, and they are damaging to the family members' relationships with each other.

What Do You Think?

What broad goals might you identify for Isobel and her family?

_____

_____

_____

_____

_____

Isobel's parents considered both Isobel's desires and their own needs and determined that the broader goals they needed to encourage were as follows:

- Isobel will follow house rules, accept the limits her parents impose on her, and contribute to the household by completing the assigned chores.

- Isobel will interact positively with her parents and siblings (e.g., voice her concerns calmly and at appropriate times, ask for things politely, express frustration without hurting others physically or emotionally, acknowledge the needs of others).

- Isobel will become involved in positive school and community activities (e.g., clubs or extracurricular activities at school, community theater) and avoid engaging in risky behavior (e.g., being out late at night and not telling anywhere where she can be found).

- Isobel will help, or at least not prevent, the home environment from being peaceful and harmonious most of the time.

In addition to considering their own goals, Isobel's parents decided that it was important to talk to Isobel—and the other members of the family—and to develop some broad goals together. Simone took Isobel out shopping for school clothes, and while they shopped, she talked to Isobel about goals Isobel had for herself and what she wanted her life to be at this time. Isobel's goal was to gain more freedom and independence from her parents. With all of these goals in mind, Isobel's parents set out to learn more about why Isobel was engaging in difficult behavior.

STEP 2: GATHERING INFORMATION

The second step in PBS is for us to gather information to better understand our children's behavior. Many parents find they can easily get this information by watching their children in different situations, talking to others who interact with their children, and recording their children's behavior.

Deciding What Information to Collect

We must select methods for gathering the types of information that will be helpful to us and determine the best way to use those methods.

What Do You Think?

What methods of information gathering might Isobel's parents use?

Watching: _____

_____

_____

Talking: _____

_____

_____

Recording: _____

_____

_____

Once Isobel and her parents determined their goals, her parents considered in what ways they could get information to better understand Isobel's behavior and needs. They decided to do the following

Watching   Isobel's parents decided to pay close attention to Isobel's behaviors and how they reacted to her behaviors, especially during the times they knew to expect problems (e.g., when assigning household chores, during dinner).

Talking   Isobel's parents sat down together and discussed where the problems usually occurred, who was usually around, and what outside circumstances were usually going on. They made a point to spend a few minutes each evening talking about how the day had gone before going to bed. They also decided to talk with some people from Isobel's school, including some of her friends and her drama teacher (this had to be done unobtrusively, so as to not offend or embarrass Isobel). Finally, they decided to talk with Isobel to see if they could get a better understanding of what she was trying to achieve through her problem behaviors.

Recording   Isobel's parents decided that if they had difficulty understanding Isobel's actions and their reactions during the most difficult circumstances, they would examine the patterns of interactions between Isobel and themselves by recording the exchanges in a journal.

Using this plan, Isobel's parents observed, discussed, and recorded the behaviors they saw for one week. This is what they learned.

In their initial attempts to understand Isobel's behavior, her parents decided that both problem behaviors happened most frequently during family times (e.g., dinner) when they gave Isobel specific demands or reminded her of the household rules. The problems were also more likely when they gave her time restrictions (e.g., "Clean up this mess immediately," "Be home by 4:00"). They decided that problem behavior occurred least frequently in the morning and when Isobel's parents did not make demands of her. They found that blatant defiance and disrespect seemed to occur at home, but not at school or in the community. They also agreed that Isobel's problem behaviors usually happened with them and only occasionally with her siblings. Problem behaviors did not usually happen when one of her parents was alone with Isobel, unless that parent was demanding a specific response from her.

Isobel's parents considered what Isobel might be getting or avoiding through her behaviors. They initially thought Isobel was refusing to do what they requested and arguing with them in order to get reactions from them. They felt that Isobel deliberately provoked their negative interactions, controlling the situation by choosing actions designed to irritate her parents and make them frustrated and angry. By challenging her parents and being difficult, Isobel was able to avoid the responsibilities she disliked. In fact, Isobel's parents often had her siblings complete Isobel's chores. They also provided Isobel with allowance and privileges regardless of her behavior because they thought of those items as entitlements. Isobel's parents realized they were making fewer demands and imposing fewer restrictions on Isobel to avoid her negative and sometimes explosive behavior.

Isobel's parents met with her drama teacher, Ms. Yost. She was very pleasant, and welcomed the opportunity to talk about Isobel. She told them that Isobel seemed to enjoy drama very much and that she was a good actress. She had not seen the problem behaviors that they described, but she told them she had noticed that Isobel really liked to be in control of her surroundings. She said that Isobel was very persuasive and did not follow other people's lead very well. She also noted that she had to be very careful when giving feedback to Isobel about her performances because Isobel would become defensive or sullen when given constructive criticism.

When Isobel's parents told her they wanted to talk to her and to better understand where she was coming from, Isobel was reluctant to participate at first. Eventually, however, Isobel did tell them that she felt that they were always directing her and judging her. Isobel said she wanted more independence and for her parents to trust her and allow her to make her own decisions. Isobel also said that she was not trying to be mean; her parents were just "driving her crazy."

Isobel's parents decided to show Isobel they respected her by asking her what she specifically wanted from them and from her family. They made it clear that by asking her these questions, they were not guaranteeing that she would get everything she wanted. Some of the things Isobel wanted were

- To get her parents to stop nagging her
- To spend more time with her friends
- To not have her actions questioned so much
- To make her own choices

Isobel's parents also asked her if there were any particular kinds of interaction with them that she enjoyed. Isobel said that she liked when Simone took her shopping and the time she and Luis spent talking while he was working in the yard. She preferred to initiate communication with her parents—perhaps because her parents often caught her at bad times or were confrontational rather than supportive.

Isobel's parents tried to broach the subject of what Isobel and her friends did in the evenings when they were out, but Isobel was evasive and defensive (e.g., saying "You know, we just hang out and whatever. I don't think you need every detail"). Her parents were frustrated about not knowing more of what Isobel did, but they decided this was not an immediate priority and they could talk to Isobel about it more later.

Looking at Isobel's behavior over the course of a whole day seemed overwhelming, so Isobel's parents decided to focus their information gathering on the occurrences at dinnertime first, hoping what they learned then would still give them insight on other times. Isobel's parents tried to make dinner a family event at least five nights per week, and it was very common for Isobel to have problems nearly every day. Isobel's parents wanted to look for patterns that might help them understand the purpose of Isobel's behaviors and understand the impact of their reactions on those patterns. They decided that maintaining a daily journal would help them to look at the situation objectively. They planned to write in the journal every day for a week. Figure 22 shows what Simone recorded over the course of a few days. As Isobel's parents continued recording, they began to see some variations in what they said to Isobel and the manner in which they said it—and how Isobel reacted in response. Once, Simone had an especially good day and was more cheerful than usual. Instead of yelling to Isobel, "Dinner's ready," she went directly to Isobel's room. She announced to Isobel in an upbeat way, "Guess what we're having for dinner? Why don't you come find out and tell us about your day." With that introduction, Isobel came to dinner more readily and was less disruptive. Isobel's parents realized that because they were expecting problems, they sometimes approached her defensively, which made things worse.

STEP 3: ANALYZING PATTERNS

The third step in the PBS process is for us to summarize what we know. That means we use the information we collected to identify patterns in the problem behavior and the circumstances surrounding it. We can summarize by writing a sentence or short paragraph that describes the patterns in our children's behavior.

What Do You Think?

Based on the information Isobel's parents collected, what patterns do you feel are affecting her behavior?

When _____

occurs, Isobel does _____

to get/avoid _____.

Isobel's parents considered their conversations and looked over the information they recorded. To help them identify patterns, they completed the finding patterns activity described in Chapter 4. Figure 23 shows how they completed the table. In addition to these immediate issues, Isobel's parents also realized how concerned they were about Isobel's actions in the evenings when out with her

Date	Notes
4/19	6:10 P.M. I called Isobel down for dinner ("Dinner's ready!"). After approximately 5 minutes, I yelled again a little louder. Isobel said, "Coming..." in a sarcastic way, but she did not come to the table. After I yelled Isobel's name, she finally came to the table and slammed herself down in her seat. Luis started talking about his day and Isobel interrupted, asking if she had to listen to him drone on again. I told Isobel to be polite. Isobel then turned to Maria and started teasing her about a boy in school she likes. Luis told Isobel that if she had nothing nice to say to just "button her mouth." Isobel picked at her dinner for approximately 10 minutes and then asked to be excused. I put her dinner aside for later.
4/20	6:20 P.M. I yelled, "Dinner!" from the kitchen. The rest of the family came and began eating. After approximately 10 minutes, Luis went to her room. She was listening to music. He said, "Your mother fixed a nice meal. The least you can do is to come eat it." Isobel replied, "I'll be there later." He said firmly, "No, you'll be there now," and turned off the music. Isobel glared at him and walked to the kitchen. She ate some of her meal and then started confronting us about why we have to nag her all of the time. We eventually just stopped talking and ate in silence.
4/22	6:05 P.M. I was putting away laundry while dinner was cooking and stopped by Isobel's room. While putting the laundry on the dresser, I asked how she was doing in school. She said, "Okay," and looked back down at her book. I told her dinner would be ready in approximately 10 minutes. At 6:20 or so, Isobel came out to the kitchen. While the other family members were arriving for dinner, I asked her to put the plates on the table. She begrudgingly complied and then sat down at the table with her arms crossed. Isobel finished her meal that night and took part in a conversation the children had about music. She did tease Aarón about his new shoes and rolled her eyes when we tried to contribute to the conversation, but it was better than most nights.

Figure 22.   Journal entries showing Isobel's behavior.

friends and her safety in general. They also recognized that they had not been consistent in their expectations or supervision. Based on this information, they developed a summary statement:

"When Isobel is asked to do something she does not want to do or is asked questions she does not want to answer, she ignores the request or yells back at us. These actions allow her to 1) avoid having to do things she does not want to do and to 2) gain control over her circumstances. This pattern may have been made worse by our inconsistent expectations and lack of supervision."

Finding Patterns: Defiance, Disrespect		
Behavior is....	**Most likely**	**Least likely**
When	Isobel is asked to do an action or chore she does not like; her parents make demands of her; her parents ask her a lot of questions	Isobel is left alone; she is doing activities she likes (e.g., shopping, going out with friends)
Where	At home, especially at the dinner table	At school
With whom	Parents; sometimes siblings	Friends; teachers
What activities	Dinner; chores	Free time; shopping
What do the behaviors....	**Get**	**Avoid**
	Control over what Isobel does and where she goes; allowance and privileges regardless of behavior	Interactions with her parents that she perceives as domineering; doing chores and adhering to rules and routines

Figure 23. Finding patterns in Isobel's behavior.

At first, Isobel's parents thought that she was creating a disruptive atmosphere in order to avoid interacting with her family. After hearing what Ms. Yost told them, however, and realizing that there was a pattern in the times that they did not have problems interacting with Isobel—it seemed more likely that Isobel was just trying to avoid the requests her parents made of her in order to try to gain control and independence. Her parents also came to recognize that their tone of voice and general approach made a difference in how Isobel reacted to them.

Testing Guesses

When we are not sure about our summary statements, we may want to test them out by changing the circumstances or outcomes surrounding the problem behavior to see if the behavior still happens—or happens as much.

Isobel's mother decided to test out her theory regarding the impact of how she approached Isobel for a couple of days. Instead of yelling dinner announcements from the kitchen, she went to speak with Isobel in person, engaged in some small talk (if Isobel was willing), and then mentioned that dinner was ready. This approach did not solve all of Isobel's challenging behaviors, but on the days these exchanges happened, Isobel seemed to come to the table more readily and eat most, if not all, of her meal.

STEP 4: DEVELOPING A PLAN

The fourth step in PBS is for us to use the understanding gained in Steps 2 and 3 to create a plan for dealing with our children's behavior.

What, Where, and When to Intervene

Prior to deciding exactly how to address our children's behavior, we need to consider what behaviors we feel we need to address right now and when and where we are going to intervene.

What Do You Think?

What behaviors should Isobel's family address in the plan (e.g., specific behaviors, general ones)?

_____

_____

When should Isobel's parents address problems (e.g., all day, certain times)?

_____

_____

Where should they focus (e.g., at home, at school, in the community)?

_____

_____

Isobel's parents decided that both problem behaviors (i.e., defiance and disrespect) were important to them and, because they often occurred together, both needed to be addressed. They decided that they wanted to make changes in their home that would make an impact on Isobel's behaviors during all of the day and every day of the week. Although their focus would be at home, Isobel's parents also needed to monitor how Isobel behaved at school and in the community. They decided to put an emphasis on dinnertime because that seemed to be a routine with chronic problems and because family dinners were important to them.

How to Intervene

Comprehensive plans for dealing with our children's behavior include a variety of strategies, including steps to prevent problems, replace problem behaviors with more appropriate behaviors, and manage the consequences of the behavior.

Preventing Problems

Once parents understand what provokes their children's behavior, they can change circumstances (e.g., avoid things that trigger problems) to help their children behave more appropriately.

What Do You Think?

What circumstances prompt Isobel's behavior?

_____

_____

_____

How can her parents change the environment to prevent problems?

Avoid difficult situations: _____

_____

_____

Make problem situations better: _____

_____

_____

Add cues to prompt appropriate behavior: _____

_____

_____

Isobel's parents determined that the circumstances that precipitated Isobel's problem behavior were as follows: when they asked her to do an action that she did not enjoy (e.g., clean her room, eat with the family), when they questioned her actions extensively (e.g., "When will you come home?"), and when they placed restrictions on her actions (e.g., curfews). Isobel's resistance to these circumstances was exacerbated by the way in which her parents approached her. Because Isobel's problem behavior occurred most when her parents asked things of her, they decided they could minimize problems by reducing and clarifying their demands. To sort out their expectations, they made a list of the responsibilities they were currently requiring of Isobel. They then crossed off the items that were not absolutely essential. Their goal was to require of Isobel only things that were necessary to create the strong, peaceful family life they desired while allowing Isobel to gain some independence. They decided to stop requiring Isobel to do the following items:

- Eat breakfast at home before school.
- Walk with her siblings to the bus stop.
- Join the family in evening walks after dinner.

Isobel's parents decided they needed to continue to require Isobel to do the following:

- Join the family for dinner (at least three times per week).
- Clean her room (at least one time per week).
- Pick up personal items from around the house (daily).
- Make curfew (8:00 P.M. weekdays, 10:00 P.M. weekends).
- Complete one household chore each day (e.g., emptying the dishwasher).

Isobel's parents also wanted to change the way in which they asked things of Isobel. They decided that making ongoing expectations clear at the outset would eliminate their having to make the demands on a regular basis. They decided that many of their expectations applied to all family members, not just Isobel, so they gathered the family together for a meeting. During the meeting, they discussed their goals for the family and asked for input from each of the children. Isobel did not really join in on the conversation, but she did sit quietly and listen as her parents and siblings talked. They came up with a single main goal: for their family to have fun together, help each other, and show they care by treating each other nicely. Isobel's parents then explained these new family expectations applied to everyone:

- Clean up after yourself by picking up your personal items each day before going to bed and cleaning your bedroom every week (at a day and time of your choice).

- Speak respectfully to each other (using a calm voice and polite words).

- Contribute to the household by taking responsibility for one household chore every day.

Isobel's parents felt that defining general expectations that applied to everyone would be less confrontational; it would make it more likely that Isobel would not feel that the expectations only involved her, an idea she had indicated during their conversation. It would also communicate to the other children what was acceptable in terms of their behavior. They wrote the expectations down and posted them on the refrigerator as a reminder.

Isobel's parents decided that they needed to change the way in which they asked Isobel to do things and that they needed to state their expectations more clearly. They sat down with Isobel and discussed the behavior changes they wanted. They told her that they realized they might have been asking her to do more than was necessary and that they were sometimes abrupt with her. They presented new, specific expectations to Isobel. They told her that she was to attend family dinners at least three times per week, that she should arrive within 5 minutes of the start of dinner and remain at the table until dinner was completed, and that she should behave in a pleasant and appropriate behavior (they came to an agreement about what this looked and sounded like).

In addition to expectations within the house, Isobel's parents decided to institute a new plan for communicating the family members' whereabouts and providing adequate supervision for the children. They posted an erasable grid on the refrigerator, put some dry erase markers with it, and listed all of the family members' names along with questions for Where, What, Who, and When. Everyone (including the parents) would be required to jot down before leaving the house where he or she was going, what he or she was doing, who he or she would be with, and when he or she intended to return to the house.

Isobel's parents also began talking with her about her interests, trying to encourage Isobel to get more involved in school and community activities. They asked her why she had discontinued her involvement in her extracurricular activities. Isobel explained she missed those activities, especially theater, but that she got tired of her parents' constantly interrogating her about them. After a lot of discussion (and prodding), Isobel agreed to try out for a play at the community theater that would require practice several times per week, and her parents agreed to let her share what has happening in the play at her own choosing rather than asking her a lot of questions every day.

Replacing Behaviors

In addition to preventing problems, we can—and should—teach our children the skills to communicate their needs and cope with difficult situations in appropriate and positive ways.

What Do You Think?

What is Isobel currently doing that is of concern?

_____

_____

_____

What would her parents like her to do instead?

_____

_____

_____

Isobel's parents thought more about Isobel's behavior and what she appeared to be gaining (and avoiding) through it. They considered strategies other people used when required to do something they did not enjoy or when they felt that they were being undeservedly controlled by someone, including how they expressed anger and frustration. They determined that they wanted Isobel to accept responsibility around the house (meet household obligations without having to be asked repeatedly) and be accountable for her activities and whereabouts.

Isobel's parents talked with her about the fact that independence requires responsibility and that when she demonstrated responsibility by meeting expectations, they would be more likely to give her greater independence. They linked meeting expectations with increasing freedom (see the next portion of this chapter—Managing Consequences).

Isobel's parents also decided that they wanted Isobel to talk to them and to her siblings calmly when expressing her concerns, likes, and dislikes. They noted that she should address others as she would like to be addressed. In addition, her parents described to Isobel the steps to appropriately voicing concerns:

1. Identify an appropriate time (when her parents are not on the telephone, working, or talking to someone else in the home).

2. In a quiet, calm voice, tell her parents that she has a concern about a topic that she would like to talk about. Remember to state her opinion, including alternative options, and to listen to her parents' response.

3. Make any further explanation or ask follow-up questions in a calm manner.

4. Continue to take turns in the conversation until all points have been made.

5. Accept her parents' decision about the issue, even if she has to agree to disagree with them.

6. Move on.

Isobel's parents realized that they had established bad habits regarding how they spoke with Isobel. They made an agreement to use themselves as models for the kind of behavior they expected from Isobel, to encourage each other to use those skills, and to acknowledge when they work things out calmly.

Managing Consequences

In order for us to replace problem behavior with more positive ways of behaving, we need to manage the outcomes of our children's behavior so that our children are rewarded for positive behavior and not problem behavior.

 ## What Do You Think?

What outcomes does Isobel achieve through her behavior?

She gets...

_____

_____

She avoids...

_____

_____

How should Isobel's parents respond to her behavior?

Reward positive behavior by...

_____

_____

Deal constructively with problem behavior by...

_____

_____

Isobel's parents thought carefully about what Isobel was getting by ignoring her responsibilities and talking rudely—sometimes explosively—to them, and they recognized that their reactions might be making the problem worse. As Isobel had become more defiant and explosive, they had made fewer requests or demands on her. She had successfully avoided doing things that her parents wanted her to do through her problem behavior. Given this understanding, Isobel's parents developed the following plan for responding to Isobel's behaviors:

- Isobel and her parents made a list of special activities and things she would like to have the chance to do. Every week that Isobel met all of the expectations listed on the refrigerator, she could choose one activity from the list. The list included items such as going to the mall or to the movies with a friend and shopping for a new article of clothing.

- Isobel and her parents also made a list of privileges that she currently had. It included things such as talking on the telephone, using the computer, and watching television. Isobel and her parents had considered these things to be rights in the past, but now they clearly established them as privileges that could be taken away.

- Isobel's access to these privileges were based on expectations established for her behavior: cleaning up after herself, speaking respectfully to her family, adhering to curfew, joining her family for dinner, completing her assigned chores, and recording her whereabouts on the dry erase chart.

Isobel's parents realized that Isobel would probably test them to see if they would follow through with the new restrictions on her behavior, especially because they had been so inconsistent with how they dealt with her in the past. They needed to remain calm and focused when dealing with Isobel and to make sure that their restrictions could be consistently enforced. Given how hard it would be to change their patterns of behavior, Isobel's parents would need to reassure each other to survive first few days (and perhaps weeks), but they believed if they adhered to the plan, they would see improvement in Isobel's behavior.

Improving Lives

In creating plans to address our children's behavior, we should periodically revisit the broader goals we were hoping to achieve and make sure we are addressing any lifestyle issues that may be having an impact on our children's actions.

What Do You Think?

What changes can be made in Isobel's life that might improve her behavior?

_____

_____

_____

_____

_____

Because Isobel is approaching the age at which she can get a part-time job, and seemed to desire great autonomy from her parents, they decided to help Isobel explore the possibilities of employment, the types of job she might enjoy, and the kind of responsibilities that working would require. Isobel's parents hoped to extend the connection between dependability and privileges to an area of interest for Isobel.

Putting the Plan in Place

Once we have created a plan to support positive behavior in our children, we need to consider how we are going to initiate and maintain the plan. We should talk with our children and other adults involved in our children's care, obtain any materials we may need, think of ways we can periodically review how well the plan is doing, and adjust or alter the plan if needed.

What Do You Think?

What steps need to be taken to put Isobel's plan into action (and who might be responsible for maintaining that plan)?

_____

_____

_____

_____

_____

Isobel's parents knew that it would be important to make their new expectations, restrictions, and access to privileges clear and to be consistent with the new rules. They also knew that to meet Isobel's growing desire for independence, they would need to connect responsibility to greater freedom. Ideas that were necessary for their plan to be successful included

- Isobel's parents worked with her to develop a written contract that specified the expectations, privileges, and consequences they had agreed upon for Isobel's behavior.

- Simone blocked out time on her calendar every Saturday afternoon to transport Isobel to the mall, to the movies, or to wherever Isobel chose for a special activity if she met her goals that week.

- Isobel's family met occasionally (every other week) to talk about how they were doing, to discuss if they were achieving their vision as a family, and to plan strategy.

- Isobel's parents agreed to meet with her after she had been successful for a few weeks to begin to establish even more opportunities for independence.

STEP 5: MONITORING RESULTS

By regularly monitoring how our children are responding to the plans in place, we can quickly address any problems that might arise and make necessary changes. Monitoring results involves tracking the replacement behaviors as well as the problem behaviors, supervising how well the plan is working, and noting all positive outcomes (even unplanned ones).

What Do You Think?

What should Isobel's parents do to monitor the results of their plan?

_____

_____

_____

_____

_____

Isobel's parents realized the importance of frequently reflecting on the plan's progress and making adjustments to the plan as needed. In addition to meeting with Isobel and the family as a whole, they decided that they needed to stay in touch with Isobel's teachers and friends through periodic informal chats. Her parents also decided to talk by themselves at least once a week so that they could be better about communicating their concerns, solving problems, and keeping consistent. With regard to Isobel, they decided to make sure to ask themselves the following questions when meeting to discuss the plan and the results:

- How has Isobel been interacting with them and the other family members?

- Has Isobel been meeting all of the expectations, including communicating her activities and whereabouts?

- Have they been following through on consequences?

- Have they offered Isobel greater freedom when she met expectations?

- Has Isobel been voicing her concerns appropriately?

- Has the overall atmosphere around the home improved?

OUTCOMES FOR ISOBEL

Isobel reluctantly accepted the new house rules and participated in family discussions about how things were going. At first, she picked up her personal belongings and completed her assigned chore only after prompted by her parents or by Maria (everyone in the home was to do this daily). Isobel then took it upon herself to become the enforcer of family chores, nagging her siblings about their rooms and belongings. This resulted in conflict for the entire family and Isobel became increasingly defensive. At a family meeting, they decided that each family member would check off on the family calendar when he or she had cleaned his or her room or completed his or her chores in order to avoid some of these unpleasant interactions.

Isobel made it to dinner a few times during the first week, but she was argumentative and rude. As a result, her privileges were revoked for the rest of the day following each of these meals. She became quite upset, shouting that her parents were crazy and could not force her to do anything. When Isobel became calm, her parents reminded her that it was important not only for her to attend dinner, but also to participate nicely in the family's conversations and to be decent to others. After a few days without privileges, Isobel changed her behavior at the dinner table. She did not talk much, but when she was spoken to, she responded. A few weeks later, when Isobel had met both dinner and cleaning expectations, her parents talked to her, acknowledged her success, and offered her an additional activity that allowed her some additional freedoms.

Isobel's parents also changed how they approached her. They often found that they had to take a deep breath and think about what they were going to say so as to not be overly directive or demanding. Isobel began to respond positively to these changes. As time went on, Isobel's parents found that although they were still having some hassles, their overall attitude toward and relationship with Isobel had improved.

To Isobel's parents' pleasant surprise, Isobel had no trouble with the system for recording their activities and whereabouts on the refrigerator (possibly because it applied to everyone and possibly because she viewed it as better than being questioned by her parents). The family found that recording these activities prompted new and more positive discussions at the dinner table as they shared their days. In addition, Isobel did get a part in the community play. Dinnertime allowed a period of sharing daily experiences, and having Isobel's family attend the play was enjoyable for everyone.

After the plan had been in place for a few months, Isobel generally did what was expected of her. She enjoyed the additional freedoms she was given when she got along with the family. There were occasional times when Isobel missed curfew or became confrontational with her parents, but after a day or two without privileges, she returned to more appropriate behaviors. The family discussions brought out several other things that were of concern to Isobel and her parents. They were able to discuss heated issues in the calm manner that they taught Isobel early on. These discussions did not always work out pleasantly, but some of them did, which was a great improvement from how things went in the past. Isobel's parents sometimes found it difficult to monitor her when she was restricted from privileges, but they agreed that it was worth the extra effort to follow through because they could see that Isobel's problem behavior was decreasing.

Overall, Isobel's parents noticed improvement in the home. They were generally more relaxed, probably because they now had a plan for dealing with Isobel's behavior. Conflict between Isobel's parents diminished because they were together in their disciplinary beliefs. Isobel's siblings commented that they wanted to spend more time together as a family, and even Isobel herself seemed to enjoy the new way the family interacted.

CHAPTER 9

Michael's Story

Michael is a 9-year-old boy who is sweet and respectful. He has a wonderful smile and is eager to listen to his mother, Deborah, his peers, and his teachers. He likes watching movies, playing board games, and constructing things out of Legos. Michael is somewhat shy; he greets people with lowered eyes and a soft voice. In addition, Michael suffers from asthma. Attacks were more frequent when he was younger, but now he has them only occasionally. He carries an inhaler and uses it when he feels out of breath during exercise or extreme weather changes.

Michael has been identified as having a learning disability, mainly in the area of reading and organization, for which he receives special services at school. He spends most of the school day in a general education classroom, but he also attends a resource room for students with specific learning disabilities during his language arts class. He struggles to keep up with the requirements in his grade level and receives after-school tutoring from his special education teacher. The tutoring seems to be helping; Michael has made progress for the first time this past year, after becoming eligible for special help. Michael does his homework after school or in the evening slowly and with effort as long as his mother sits with him and provides him assistance. However, these homework sessions are often long and frustrating for both of them.

Michael's parents have been divorced since Michael was 5 years old. Deborah has primary custody of Michael. She is a nurse in a local clinic. She is patient, loving, and calm. She tries to make Michael's life as easy for him as possible. She also tries to fulfill both the mother and father parental roles and overcompensates for the challenges in Michael's life by being extremely lenient in her discipline with Michael. This overemphasis on Michael's needs often means that she neglects her own (e.g., she rarely spends time with her friends). She apologizes to Michael often and feels guilty that she cannot provide everything for him. Michael's father, Phillip, sees him on occasion but is not involved in Michael's daily life or in the decisions surrounding his upbringing. Phillip is passive and easygoing, very similar in personality to Michael.

Deborah works a regular 9-to-4 schedule at the clinic and so is able to get Michael off to school in the morning and be home by 5:30 to prepare dinner and eat with Michael. Having dinner together is very important to the two of them. In the evenings after his homework has been completed, Michael plays on the computer, watches television, and creates elaborate structures with Legos. Michael and Deborah usually spend their weekends together. Michael is happy to help her with chores and errands. He rarely chooses to be in social situations, but when he is with other children (e.g., at school, at the local park), he is liked and included by other children. Michael feels most comfortable in his home surrounded by things that are familiar to him. He does not enjoy changes or time limits, and he resists trying new things.

Michael's biggest problem is around transitions. It is very difficult for him to leave one activity for another. When he was younger, he was always the last one to come out of preschool or the last to leave a play date or birthday party. He was always late to engagements because he dawdled instead of getting dressed and ready to go. Deborah always seemed to indulge him at these times and did not see his tardiness as a big problem. She felt that as the child of a single parent, Michael needed all the ease of life and patience that she could give him. When she worked part-time, this behavior of Michael's did not interfere very much with her day. She reasoned that he took a long time to go from one place or activity to another because he was young and engrossed in the activity of the moment. However, since she began working full-time, his behavior has begun to interfere with the routine of the household, especially during the weekday mornings.

School mornings are particularly problematic. On a typical day, Deborah goes to Michael's room and wakes him up approximately an hour before they need to leave. She tells him in a friendly way that it is time to get up, then goes to take her shower. After her shower, she returns to his room to find him still asleep in bed. She then turns on his radio and tells him he can listen to one more song, then he has to get up and take a shower himself. She usually goes to the kitchen to make coffee and comes back to his room approximately 5 minutes later. Michael is still in bed. At this point, Deborah begins to get annoyed. She sometimes shakes Michael, telling him, "Get up this instant." She goes back to her room to get dressed, and when she returns she finds Michael still in bed.

By this point, Deborah is anxious about being late for work. She raises her voice, frantically pulling Michael out of bed and walking him to the bathroom. She pushes him toward the shower, shouting, "You have to hurry or we will be late for the carpool!" or threatening him, "If you're late, I'm not driving you to school today." Approximately 30 minutes would have passed since Deborah first told Michael it was time to wake up. When Michael finally gets in the shower, Deborah prepares his breakfast. She feels neglectful if Michael does not eat well before school. After 15 minutes, Michael finally comes down, dressed for school; by then it is too late to catch the carpool.

Several days each week, Michael misses his carpool to school. Deborah ends up driving him to school while Michael eats his breakfast in the car. When Deborah confronts him about the morning chaos, he apologizes and says he will try to do better. Most mornings, Deborah ends up feeling resentful and agitated and is late for work as well. Her supervisor at work has begun to comment on her frequent tardiness, and the other parents involved in the carpool are tired of coming to pick Michael up, only to have Deborah tell them that Michael is not ready yet and she will drive him to school instead. Michael's mother has come to dread weekday mornings; she sees no good solutions to the difficulties she faces every day.

STEP 1: ESTABLISHING GOALS

The first step in PBS is for us to identify goals, define and prioritize specific behaviors of concern, and establish larger, lifestyle goals for our children and families.

Defining the Problem Behavior(s)

Behaviors of concern must be defined clearly. We should make the definitions as specific as necessary to ensure that the behaviors would be identifiable to people who have even casual interactions with our children. We also want to estimate the frequency (how often), duration (how long), and seriousness (how intense) of the behaviors at the outset, so we will be able to assess the change later. Remember, behavior is anything a person says or does.

What Do You Think?

Given what is going on with Michael and Deborah, what would you identify as his primary behavior(s) of concern?

Behavior(s): _____

_____

_____

Description: _____

_____

_____

Frequency, duration, and seriousness: _____

_____

_____

Deborah recognizes that Michael has difficulties with transitions throughout the day, but her largest concern is the transition of getting out of bed and ready for school. She refers to this behavior as dawdling.

Behavior: Dawdling.

Description: Michael remains in his bed and ignores Deborah's specific requests to get ready in the morning. Michael whines, pulls blankets over his head, and turns toward the wall; these behaviors seem to get worse as his mother repeatedly states her requests.

Frequency, duration, and seriousness: Michael misses carpool due to dawdling two to three times per week, which means that Deborah must drive him to school and arrive late to work.

Determining if the Behavior Is Really a Problem

Part of identifying goals is for us to decide whether the behaviors of concern are severe enough to warrant addressing them. Consider the Big Ds. Are the behaviors dangerous, destructive, disruptive, disgusting, or developmentally inappropriate?

What Do You Think?

Look at the definition of Michael's behaviors of concern and decide whether his behavior is really a problem according to the ideas behind the Big Ds.

Dangerous: _____

_____

Destructive: _____

_____

Disruptive: _____

_____

Disgusting: _____

_____

Developmentally inappropriate: _____

_____

Deborah considered only two Big Ds to be a concern (see Table 5). To Deborah, it was clear that Michael's behavior was not dangerous, destructive, or disgusting. She was not sure about whether it was developmentally inappropriate, but

Table 5. Michael's Big Ds for dawdling

Disruptive	Michael's refusal to follow directions results in Deborah becoming frustrated and resorting to yelling and using physical force to get him out of bed. This behavior interferes with the harmony of the home and starts the day in a negative way. It also may affect Deborah's job if she is repeatedly late to work.
Developmentally inappropriate	Deborah is not sure, but she thinks that accepting a responsibility such as getting ready for school should be expected of a child Michael's age.

her discussions with co-workers led her to believe that Michael was having a much more difficult time getting out of bed and ready for school than most children of a similar age.

Establishing Broad Goals

In addition to defining behaviors of concern, we also want to consider what broader goals we want to achieve for our children and families. Broad goals go beyond just stopping a problem behavior and include things like improving relationships, building opportunities, and maintaining emotional well-being.

What Do You Think?

What broad goals might you identify for Michael and Deborah?

_____

_____

_____

_____

_____

Deborah thought about the goals she wanted, not just for her and Michael's morning routine, but for their overall lives. She identified the following goals:

- Michael will develop independence and personal responsibility for getting himself ready for school in the morning.

- Michael and Deborah will arrive on time for work, school, and their other engagements on a consistent basis.

- Michael and Deborah will have more peace and less conflict in their relationship, especially in the morning.

- Deborah will spend more time attending to her own personal needs, including going out in the evenings with friends.

STEP 2: GATHERING INFORMATION

The second step in PBS is for us to gather information to better understand our children's behavior. Many parents find they can easily get this information by watching their children in different situations, talking to others who interact with their children, and recording their children's behavior.

Decide What Information to Collect

We must select methods for gathering the types of information that will be helpful to us and determine the best way to use those methods.

What Do You Think?

What methods of information gathering might Deborah use?

Watching: _____

_____

_____

Talking: _____

_____

_____

Recording: _____

_____

_____

Deborah realized that even though she and Michael were the only ones involved in the problem behavior, she would benefit from the input and involvement of others. She recognized that a lengthy information-gathering process was not realistic given her demands as a single parent and that such a process probably was not necessary given the circumstances. She decided that it would be sufficient to select strategies that focused on talking and watching, rather than recording, in order to gain a better understanding of Michael's behavior. Her plan was as follows:

Watching   Pay attention to bedtime and transitions, especially weekday morning routines to see what might be affecting Michael's behavior, including the interactions between Deborah and Michael (e.g., what she says and does and how he responds). Consider things such as how much sleep Michael gets the night before and who drives him to school (i.e., Deborah or a carpool parent). Observe how Michael behaves on weekend and holiday mornings when they are not getting up to go to work or school. Use the time spent on driving to work to consider the behaviors observed while interacting during the morning routine.

Talking   Deborah decided to talk with Michael and got his input regarding the morning routine, as well as the impact of his behavior on his experiences in the carpool and at school. She spoke to Michael's teacher to see if there were any situations at school that might make him resist going to school. She also got input from the other parents in the carpool regarding what happens on the ride to school. After gathering all of the information, Deborah planned to talk with a good friend to help develop an understanding of the variables affecting Michael's behavior.

Recording Deborah decided not to record any of her observations because she thought she would be able to understand Michael's behavior by simply paying attention, talking through the observations with a friend, and giving herself time to step back from her frustration and consider the patterns and purpose(s) of Michael's behavior.

When Deborah talked to Michael, he told her that things were fine at school; however, after some prodding, he admitted that he just did not really like being there. When she asked him why, he said that he did not really like having to go to the "boom boom" class (his term for the special education class) because the class was stupid and was not really helping him. When she asked him about weekday mornings, he told her that he did not know why he had a problem getting ready for school; he just knew that he would rather just stay home with her.

Deborah also talked to his teacher, Ms. Miller, who told her that although other children seemed to like Michael, he chose to stay by himself and not to be included in many of the social activities during lunch and recess. Ms. Miller also said that Michael did not assert himself and the children did not seem to notice him. He resisted joining the activities and seemed more comfortable watching instead of participating. When Ms. Miller really pushed him to do things with other children, they welcomed him and he seemed to have a good time as well. She also told Deborah that he needed encouragement to get his school assignments completed in class and she frequently had to remind him to get busy. Ms. Miller said that she would like for Michael to work harder without having so many reminders. She also suggested that Deborah talk to the special education teacher, Mrs. Sharp.

Deborah told Mrs. Sharp about Michael's comments regarding her class. She told Deborah that although she was fond of Michael and that he tried hard and never caused trouble, she noticed that he sometimes had difficulty making the transition from his general education class to hers and was often late or disorganized. Mrs. Sharp explained that during the time that Michael is in her class, she has 12 other students from three different grade levels. She tries to personalize the curriculum to meet each student's specific needs, but she is unable to give them much personalized attention. Mrs. Sharp told Deborah that the time spent with Michael in tutoring after school was very productive and that extra personal time was largely responsible for his academic progress this year. They agreed to meet at another time to talk in greater detail about Michael's academic progress and how Deborah could best help during homework time to avoid the conflicts.

The other parents in the carpool told Deborah that Michael was usually rather quiet on the drive to school, but—when the children or adults interacted with him—he responded. They assumed that he just had trouble waking up in the mornings and was too tired to interact. The parents seemed to think that their children liked Michael.

Deborah looked closely at Michael's bedtime and morning routines. She found nothing unusual about bedtime and Michael slept well at night; Michael usually got approximately 10 hours of sleep each night and his bedtime routine was consistent and happy. After dinner, they generally worked on Michael's homework, took the dog for a walk, and watched television for approximately 30 minutes. Deborah noted that although Michael did not enjoy doing homework, and they often got so frustrated that they yelled at each other, Michael never gave up and always completed the assignments. After homework, Michael brushed his teeth and Deborah tucked him into bed. Observing the morning routine, however, Deborah noticed that they usually experienced the same negative cycle of interactions. Deborah would tell him it was time to wake up, Michael would stay asleep, she reminded, he stayed, she yelled, he ignored, she pulled him out of bed, he eventually took his shower but as slowly as possible, and then she shouted and threatened until he was ready for school and she was angry and frustrated.

After careful consideration, Deborah noticed that on mornings when she was driving the carpool, Michael seemed to need fewer reminders and she did not usually become so frustrated. She also noticed that on Sundays, when they had to get up to go to church, Michael had some difficulty getting up on time but not nearly as much as on school days. On Sundays, it usually took her only a few reminders and prompts to get ready. She did not have to wake him up quite so early because he generally showered on Saturday evening. She usually prepared a big hot breakfast for the two of them, or sometimes they went out to breakfast on their way to church. While getting out of bed, Michael often begged Deborah to let him stay with her in the main church service rather than going to the youth class with the children his age. On the days when Deborah agreed to let him sit with her, he usually got ready more easily.

STEP 3: ANALYZING PATTERNS

The third step in the PBS process is for us to summarize what we know. That means we use the information we collected to identify patterns in the problem behavior and the circumstances surrounding it. We can summarize by writing a sentence or short paragraph that describes the patterns in our children's behavior.

 ## What Do You Think?

Based on the information Deborah collected, what patterns do you feel are affecting his behavior?

When _____

occurs, Michael does _____

to get/avoid _____ .

Deborah discussed with a friend what she learned from her conversations and observations of the circumstances around the bedtime and morning routines. Deborah considered the patterns in Michael's behavior and made some conclusions. His dawdling was most likely to take place on school mornings but occurred with less intensity on days when Deborah drove the carpool. It was not as likely to take place on days when there was less time pressure and when the day's activities were to take place around the home or with the two of them together. Michael's dawdling seemed to get him more time and attention from Deborah, and he often got to ride to school with Deborah as a result. It helped him avoid engaging in the unpleasant transition from bed to school.

Deborah realized that Michael was having a lot of problems and concerns with school and that he may be trying to avoid those unpleasant situations. After considering the patterns in circumstances and behavior, Deborah created a summary about his problem behavior:

"When I give Michael instructions about getting ready for school, he ignores me to get increasingly more attention from me and to avoid (or put off) having to go to school. This problem in getting ready seems to relate to social and academic difficulties at school."

STEP 4: DEVELOPING A PLAN

The fourth step in PBS is for us to use the understanding gained in Steps 2 and 3 to create a plan for dealing with our children's behavior.

What, Where, and When to Intervene

Prior to deciding exactly how to address our children's behavior, we need to consider what behaviors we feel we need to address right now and when and where we are going to intervene.

What Do You Think?

What behaviors should Deborah address in the plan (e.g., specific behaviors, general ones)?

_____

_____

When should Deborah address problems (e.g., all day, certain times)?

_____

_____

Where should Deborah focus (e.g., at home, at school, in the community)?

_____

_____

Although Michael had problems with transitions in general, Deborah felt that teaching Michael the importance of getting ready on time during school mornings was the primary behavior of concern.

How to Intervene

Comprehensive plans for dealing with our children's behavior include a variety of strategies, including steps to prevent problems, replace problem behaviors with more appropriate behaviors, and manage the consequences of the behavior.

Preventing Problems

Once parents understand what provokes their children's behavior, they can change circumstances (e.g., avoid things that trigger problems) to help their children behave more appropriately.

What Do You Think?

What circumstances prompt Michael's behavior?

_____

_____

_____

How can Deborah change the environment to prevent problems?

Avoid difficult situations: _____

_____

_____

Make problem situations better: _____

_____

_____

Add cues to prompt appropriate behavior: _____

_____

_____

Michael had problems in the morning before school, especially when someone other than Deborah would be driving him to school. Here are the strategies Deborah came up with to try to prevent the problems:

- Meet with Mrs. Sharp and Ms. Miller to determine whether the needs associated with Michael's learning disability could be supported in his general education language arts class rather than going to the special education resource room.

- Help both teachers to develop goals and plans encouraging Michael to develop friendships with some other children and complete his schoolwork more quickly (e.g., pairing him with students who have similar interests, having a classmate help him get organized for lessons).

- Talk with the Sunday school teacher to make sure she understands Michael's limitations in reading and knows how to support and include him effectively. Share the strategies learned from Michael's school.

- With Ms. Miller's assistance, encourage Michael to develop relationships with some other students in school and invite them over to play or get Michael involved in activities with them outside of school.

- Plan social activities periodically with the children in the carpool.

- Provide personalized attention toward Michael when he is not under time demands, such as engaging in activities on the weekends.

- Have Michael take his shower at night in order to free up time in the morning.

- Set up a clear routine and expectations for the morning. For example: Michael's alarm will go off at 7:30 A.M.; Deborah will come in for 5 minutes to make sure he gets out of bed; Michael will get dressed, comb his hair, and brush his teeth; and Michael will be downstairs ready for breakfast with Deborah at 8:00 A.M.

Replacing Behaviors

In addition to preventing problems, we can—and should—teach our children the skills to communicate their needs and cope with difficult situations in appropriate and positive ways.

What Do You Think?

What is Michael currently doing that is of concern?

_____

_____

_____

What would Deborah like him to do instead?

_____

_____

_____

Michael took so much time to get ready for school that he was consistently late and often required Deborah to take time out of her day and drive him to school. Michael seemed to like getting Deborah to drive him and her nagging resulted in more attention from her, even though the attention was often negative.

Deborah wanted Michael to get out of bed and ready for school with limited direction from her. She also wanted him to ask for and plan time with her appropriately (e.g., "I know we are in a hurry now, but could we do a board game together tonight?"). In addition, all the adults involved in Michael's life agreed that he needed to develop skills for initiating and following through with tasks and for interacting with other children.

Managing Consequences

In order for us to replace problem behavior with more positive ways of behaving, we need to manage the outcomes of our children's behavior so that our children are rewarded for positive behavior and not problem behavior.

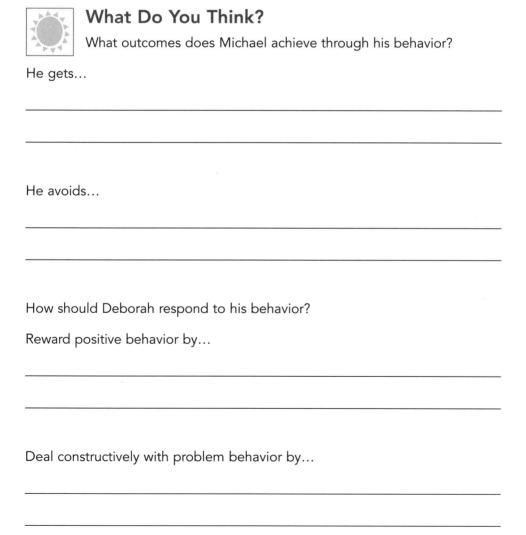

What Do You Think?

What outcomes does Michael achieve through his behavior?

He gets...

_____

_____

He avoids...

_____

_____

How should Deborah respond to his behavior?

Reward positive behavior by...

_____

_____

Deal constructively with problem behavior by...

_____

_____

The following elements will be put in place to reward positive behavior:

- Deborah will praise and encourage Michael when she finds him getting ready independently (e.g., "Wow, that was fast; you're really rolling this morning"). She will make it a point to catch him getting ready and say something nice as often as possible, especially during the first few weeks of the new plan.

- If Michael gets ready on time as described in the prevention section, Deborah will make him a hot breakfast and do a 10-minute activity (e.g., a game, a walk) with him before sending him off to school.

- If Michael gets ready on time every day for a week, he may choose an activity to do with Deborah on the weekend and Deborah will drive him to school on an additional day the following week, picking a day that does not conflict with her work schedule.

- The other carpool parents will encourage their children to greet Michael warmly when they pick him up and will keep a favorite toy of Michael's in their cars for him.

- Mrs. Sharp will meet with Michael each week to discuss his progress on his goals, providing feedback on how rapidly he is completing work and on his interactions with peers. If he makes progress each week, she will give him a homework pass, which he can use to opt out of one of his assignments during the next week.

These actions will be taken to deal with problem behavior:

- When Michael does not meet the expectations that Deborah explained to him and delays getting ready, she will limit giving him her attention until he is doing what he is supposed to do (e.g., not trying to cajole him or nag him to hurry up). This same approach will be used at school.

- If Michael is not ready on time, he will be given a granola or cereal bar to eat in the car for breakfast and he will be ushered out to the carpool in whatever condition he is in at the time.

Improving Lives

In creating plans to address our children's behavior, we should periodically revisit the broader goals we were hoping to achieve and make sure we are addressing any lifestyle issues that may be having an impact on our children's actions.

What Do You Think?

What changes can be made in Michael's life that might improve his behavior?

_____

_____

_____

_____

_____

Deborah felt that Michael's life could be improved by developing relationships with other people, especially other children. At that time, she was the only person with whom he chose to interact. She decided to pay more attention to developing relationships with other families so that she and Michael might both develop friendships. She realized that other than church functions, the two of them usually spent their time out of work and school at home together. She decided that together they would attend at least two social activities each month as an effort to develop more friendships in both of their lives.

Putting the Plan in Place

Once we have created a plan to support positive behavior in our children, we need to consider how we are going to initiate and maintain the plan. We should talk with our children and other adults involved in our children's care, obtain any materials we may need, think of ways we can periodically review how well the plan is doing, and adjust or alter the plan if needed.

What Do You Think?

What steps need to be taken to put Michael's plan into action (and who might be responsible for maintaining that plan)?

_____

_____

_____

_____

_____

Deborah spent some time on a Saturday afternoon talking about her concerns and explaining the plan to Michael. Michael was worried about remembering the new expectations, and Deborah agreed to remind him of them first thing in the morning each day and again at bedtime. They also discussed special activities they could do together and children with whom Michael was interested in developing friendships. Deborah contacted Ms. Miller, who confirmed that one of the children Michael listed would be likely to develop a friendship with him if both children were encouraged to do so. After two identified a particular child, Ms. Miller agreed to contact the parents of the boy and see if it would be acceptable for Deborah to have their telephone number. Once Deborah had the contact information, she telephoned the boy's parents and made plans to get the boys together after school or on the weekend. She also decided to talk to the other parents in the carpool to let them know her plans, just in case Michael came to the car one day looking like he just got out of bed. She gave the other parents small packs of Legos to keep in their cars and asked them to make a point of greeting Michael when they picked him up.

Deborah spoke again with Michael's teachers and asked them to reconsider how Michael receives special services, revise his academic goals, and discuss how they could communicate with each other to make sure the plan was working. They recorded the specific strategies on a parent conference form and Deborah got an extra copy to share with Michael's Sunday school teacher.

STEP 5: MONITORING RESULTS

By regularly monitoring how our children are responding to the plans in place, we can quickly address any problems that might arise and make necessary changes. Monitoring results involves tracking the replacement behaviors as well as the problem behaviors, supervising how well the plan is working, and noting all positive outcomes (even unplanned ones).

What Do You Think?

What should Deborah do to monitor the results of her plan?

_____

_____

_____

_____

_____

Deborah decided that when she arrived at work, she would make note on her calendar of how that day's morning had gone. She wanted to keep track of how well the plan was working and to be as consistent as possible in implementing it. She recorded whether Michael was ready on time and if he got his breakfast and special activity. She also noted Michael's play dates with his friends on her calendar. She asked Mrs. Sharp to e-mail a weekly report on how Michael was doing at school and made a point to check in with the carpool parents on how well Michael was interacting with them and their children. Every Sunday morning over breakfast, she and Michael talked about the events and activities going on at home and school.

OUTCOMES FOR MICHAEL

Michael responded well to the new plan. He began to get out of bed more quickly and was ready to go to school in a reasonable amount of time. On the first day they started the plan, Deborah popped into his room a couple of times while he was getting ready and made positive comments to him about his progress. On the second day, however, Deborah received a telephone call from her brother while Michael was getting ready. The call threw off the time schedule and, even though Michael had earned a special activity, they did not have time to do it. Deborah told Michael they could do an activity together after school, but Michael was rather upset when he left with the carpool. The next day, although Michael still got ready to leave on time, Deborah had to prompt him several times. Michael did not have time to eat a hot breakfast and told Deborah that the plan was stupid and she did not really want to do activities with him anyway.

Deborah reflected on the influence of the telephone call on Michael's behavior and her consistency in using the plan. She realized that there were often distractions in the morning (e.g., telephone calls, chores to be completed) and that these distractions made her less attentive to Michael's needs. Therefore, she decided to minimize such distractions by not answering the telephone, leaving nonessential chores for another time, and attending to her personal needs (e.g., taking a shower) the night before when possible.

Deborah and Michael's teachers met to talk about the educational changes that could be made at school. They decided that Mrs. Sharp could show Ms. Miller some special strategies to help Michael during the language arts class and Mrs. Sharp could continue to give Michael personalized assistance during after-school tutoring, which seemed to be the most effective intervention. Michael was able to stay in his general education language arts class once his teachers made some accommodations (e.g., a limited number of spelling words, a reading buddy to help him, the ability to take books home for his mother to read to him the day before the books would be read in class). Ms. Miller deliberately paired Michael with other students and encouraged him to interact with his peers more.

Michael's teachers gave Deborah some suggestions for the best ways to help him with his homework. They changed Michael's homework assignments to make them reviews of the lessons he had already learned at school so that homework time was used as a reinforcement of his skills. They suggested that Michael read books that were several grade levels below his educational ability so that Michael would begin to view reading as an easy and fun task to do. They found some high-interest, low-level chapter books that were relatively easy for Michael to read but would not look out of place among peer-centered reading groups.

Deborah's attempts to establish a friendship for Michael with one of his school classmates never really succeeded. One set of carpool parents, however, ran into some financial difficulties and began to work longer hours. Deborah agreed to watch their son on the afternoons her own work schedule permitted, something she usually would not have done but for the fact that she was trying to encourage Michael to develop friendships. She was concerned at first that Michael would view this change as her way of limiting their special time together, but although Michael was not initially thrilled, he agreed to this new adjustment. Deborah would participate in some of the activities and games with the boys, then make up an excuse that required her to leave the game and withdraw from the boys as they played. The boys quickly became friends and began looking forward to their afternoons together. As their friendship grew, Michael started going over to the boy's house in the evenings, giving his mother free time of her own and even opportunities to get out of the house.

In general, Michael and Deborah were both happier, and their morning routines went much more smoothly. Michael said that he enjoyed school more, Michael and Deborah found homework to be more pleasant, and Michael had a new friend. Deborah was able to take some time for herself, strengthen her own friendships, and take part in activities she enjoyed.

Enhancing Lives Through Positive Behavior Support

Making the Process Work for Families

Sections I and II described how to use PBS to gain a better understanding of why children behave as they do and how to develop practical strategies to encourage more appropriate behaviors. The stories in Section III included detailed descriptions of the PBS steps, as well as some larger considerations that families face when addressing behavior concerns. Included in those three sections were various examples showing children with very different behavioral concerns and family circumstances. In summary, we learned how to

1. *Define* problem behaviors and the skills our children need to replace those problem behaviors

2. *Establish goals* for changing our children's behavior and improving our children's and our families' lives in general

3. *Gather information* to better understand why our children are behaving the way they are

4. *Summarize patterns* and include the circumstances that may be affecting our children's behavior and the outcomes the behaviors achieve

5. *Develop strategies* to prevent behavior problems, teach more appropriate behaviors, and effectively manage the consequences of both positive and problem behavior

6. *Monitor results* to ensure that the strategies are working and that appropriate adjustments are made when they are needed

PBS is an important foundation for our approach to parenting and a framework that can guide how we interact with our children. While reading and doing the exercises in this book, it may have become evident to us that the principles and process of PBS may be useful not only for children with difficult behavior, but also for every family member. This creative problem-solving process can benefit any individual who wants to change his or her behavior or life in a productive way.

Whereas PBS may seem like an optimal way of dealing with behavior, we may have read the preceding three sections with a certain amount of skepticism. Skepticism is good because it is always beneficial to question new ideas. We may have a number of concerns about how to make PBS work in our families and lives. These concerns might take the form of statements such as:

- "This whole process seems ridiculously cumbersome, especially if I have to do it every time a problem arises."

- "What am I supposed to do when more than one of my children are having behavior problems?"

- "PBS seems to be focused on fixing problems. Does that mean we should just wait around for our kids to start having trouble?"

- "We can't always be around. Shouldn't our children take responsibility for their own behavior?"

- "Of course I know what I should do, but it is so hard to be consistent."

- "I try to follow the plan, but my family and friends undermine my efforts."

The goals of Section IV are to 1) describe how to integrate PBS into our families and lives and 2) to address some of the preceding concerns so that we can overcome obstacles and use PBS as efficiently and effectively at possible. Section IV is divided into two chapters. Chapter 10 provides ideas on how to create a positive family structure and solve problems associated with particular routines or situations, thereby integrating PBS in our homes. Chapter 11 focuses on making PBS succeed and addresses helping our children to become responsible for themselves, using the PBS process to help us change our own behavior, and finding ways to work effectively with everyone in our children's and families' lives to create positive change.

CHAPTER 10

Integrating Positive Behavior Support into Family Life

As illustrated in the preceding sections, PBS is an effective approach for understanding and resolving problems with children's behavior. However, PBS is not just for individual children. PBS has been used more broadly in an effort to improve the behavior of entire groups of people, and this has been demonstrated best in schoolwide PBS. Traditional approaches to school discipline have often been reactive and increasingly punitive, sometimes resulting in suspension or alternative placements for children with behavior problems. In contrast, schoolwide PBS has been used to create a more positive climate in schools and to improve the behavior of entire student populations through its collaborative, proactive, and problem-solving approach. The schools using this approach have experienced fewer discipline referrals, better social and academic achievement, and generally a more comfortable environment for students and faculty (for more information, see the Bibliography at the back of the book).

Although we would probably not want to structure our homes the same way schools are structured, the lesson we can take away from schoolwide PBS is that the principles can be used to improve how groups of people function. This may be especially true for families. If adapted to fit the unique needs and priorities of family life, PBS principles and processes can be used with the entire household to minimize problems and improve home life in general.

The reason PBS offers such promise for families is because it is a flexible, problem-solving framework that can be implemented in essentially any situation to guide and evaluate how we address behavior. It is important to note, however, that PBS neither encompasses everything we need to know about being good parents nor substitutes for the wisdom provided in parenting books regarding how to design our homes and address the issues we face with our children (see the Parenting Resources section of the Bibliography). Instead, PBS should be viewed as a way to integrate and choose among all the different ideas to which we are exposed. PBS provides a heuristic—or framework—for making smart decisions given our families' circumstances, needs, priorities, and goals.

Chapter 10 demonstrates how to apply the principles of PBS (using the structure of schoolwide PBS as a guideline) to family homes. This topic cannot possibly be given the attention it deserves within one chapter but instead provides a general structure and some preliminary ideas. The chapter segments provide guidance in examining how to arrange homes, respond to children's behavior, and use the PBS process to resolve problems associated with specific situations or routines. This chapter also provides a few examples to clarify each of those areas.

STRUCTURING OUR HOMES

Applying PBS to the whole family may seem like a tremendous challenge, even more complicated than applying the process to the behavior of individual children. On the contrary, focusing on the entire family is actually more manageable and efficient in the long run. Rather than trying to remedy individual problems as they become apparent, we can make holistic changes that benefit the entire family. We do not have to wait until our homes feel chaotic or our children are driving us crazy; we can be proactive in how we organize our lives and interact with our children. When we make some realistic changes to our environment and how we address behavior difficulties, we are able to prevent a large proportion of problem behavior from ever occurring and respond more efficiently when problems do arise. There are three ways that we can integrate PBS into our families' lives:

1. Establish a family vision and clear, consistent expectations for behavior.

2. Structure our homes to support and encourage those expectations.

3. Respond to behavior in ways that encourage positive behavior and discourage problem behavior.

Establishing a Family Vision and Expectations

Clarifying goals and expectations for children's behavior has been found to be critical for improving behavior in schools (as well as with individual children). The same idea is true for families; we must know what we want if we are going to achieve it. The first step in integrating PBS into our homes is to determine how we want our families to function, asking questions such as

- "What is important to us as a family?"
- "How do we see ourselves as a family?"
- "What principles guide our actions?"
- "What do we like about our family?"
- "What would we like to change?"

In defining our vision for our family, we summarize answers to these questions into a statement that describes what we perceive to be a successful family. For example, the statement might say that we want to be happy, healthy, and productive; that we want to live peacefully together; or that we want to strive to be our best.

Our vision is a statement of purpose; it defines for us who our family is and provides a guidepost on which we can assess our satisfaction with our lives and identify concerns. Therefore, our vision should be determined with input from the entire family—not just the adults in the family—and take into consideration our unique characteristics and needs (e.g., the ages of our children, community in which we live, our personal values and needs).

Based on this vision, we can establish expectations for behavior in our families. As explained in Chapter 5, children sometimes misbehave because they are confused as to what is expected of them or their attention is not focused on what they should be doing. When families clarify their expectations (also called rules), the expectations can help to guide actions and set limits for all family members. The expectations should be broad and apply to everyone in the house, the parents as well as the children, in almost every situation. These expectations should state the behaviors we desire, rather than just the behaviors that should be avoided, and describe each behavior in clear terms so that all family members understand what is expected. For example, a family's expectations may be "As a member in this family, you will 1) be kind and respectful to other people and 2) take responsibility for yourself and your things."

It is important for us to define exactly what behaviors we mean by our expectations. In order to specify these behaviors, we may ask ourselves questions, such as "What must family members say or do to follow the rules?" and "What might family members do to break the rules?" Table 6 gives examples of house rules and how they might be defined.

In addition to the broad expectations that apply to all family members in most circumstances, we may need to clarify to our children what it means to follow a rule in particular circumstances—especially circumstances that can be difficult for the entire family. Our expectations for behavior will certainly vary based on where we are and what we are doing, and these variations

Table 6. Examples of house rules and definitions

Expectations	Definition
Be kind and respectful to others.	Listen when other people are talking to you (e.g., look at them, be quiet, answer their questions, do as you are asked).
	Communicate with words, not your hands (e.g., do not hit or shove, do not grab things from others).
	Use a calm voice and polite words (e.g., say "please" and "thank you"; do not threaten, insult, yell, or whine).
Take responsibility for yourself and your things.	Clean up after yourself (e.g., put your shoes, schoolwork, and jackets away; place dirty clothes in the hamper; clear off the table when finished eating; clean up your room periodically).
	Complete your homework and daily chores (e.g., take out the trash, collect laundry, help prepare meals).
	Admit when you make a mistake and accept the consequences of your actions (e.g., apologize right away, offer to correct your mistake).

should be clearly explained. For example, we might want to define what it means to be kind and respectful when

- At the dinner table (e.g., using the eating utensils appropriately, remaining seated at the table until everyone has finished his or her meal, clearing the plates off the table when finished eating)

- Getting ready in the morning (e.g., sharing the available time in the bathroom with other family members, waking up early enough to catch the bus to school)

- On family outings (e.g., talking quietly when in a restaurant, staying with family members at a store, responding politely to greetings when out with family members)

It is not sufficient for us to merely establish house rules; the rules need to be taught. We can teach the rules by making sure that all family members know what the rules are and what the rules mean and by providing opportunities for our family to discuss and practice the rules as needed (this is especially important in families with young children). For example, we might discuss the rules at the dinner table or during a family meeting and ask our children to give us some examples of actions associated with following the rules and actions that would constitute rule breaking. As our children become older, discussions might include more complicated issues, such as family cooperation, relationships, and moral dilemmas. It is often beneficial for us to write down our family's vision and/or expectations and post them in a common place (e.g., on the refrigerator) for all the family members to see. If there are small children in the family, they may understand the list better if pictures are posted to illustrate the rules (e.g., a picture of two hands holding each other as a symbol to remind children to be gentle).

Possibly the most important way to teach expectations is for us to demonstrate the expectations ourselves—making sure we follow our rules and model the behaviors we want to promote in our families. Modeling behavior that aligns with the house rules is a subtle way of pointing the rules out. For example, a parent might say things such as, "I had better get my chores done before I watch television" or "I lost my temper and yelled, breaking a house rule; next time, I will walk away and calm down before talking to you about what is bothering me."

After we have taught the rules, we must refer to and discuss the rules often and praise family members when they follow the rules. It is especially important to review the rules just before entering situations that we know to be difficult for our families.

Organizing Our Space and Time

Once we have established and taught the expectations we have for our families, we need to consider whether, or in what ways, our households are organized to promote and consistently follow through with our expectations. In

Activity: Family Vision and Expectations

What is your vision for your family?	
What expectations do you have for your family?	**What do those expectations mean in terms of what your family members should and should not do?**

In what ways might your expectations vary across circumstances?

How will you communicate and teach these expectations to your family?

order to help achieve our vision, we may need to reorganize our physical space or change our routines to better meet our families' needs, encourage positive interactions, and/or minimize issues that may provoke problem behavior (e.g., distractions, clutter). Making household adjustments may help us prevent many of the problems we deal with on a regular basis. Whereas every family will operate differently and have their own particular style, there are two general areas that can be modified to help manage and organize every household: space and time.

Space

A simple, but not always obvious, consideration in organizing our households is how we arrange our physical space, namely the surroundings and belongings (e.g., furniture and living space) within our homes. When organizing our space, we may need to consider whether the way in which things are placed around the house encourages or discourages following of the expectations. Depending on our families' priorities, our home environments may be very structured or very relaxed. We might want to consider these questions:

- Are there storage places designated for items that are used every day (e.g., bins for toys, hooks for book bags and purses, boxes for important papers, racks or baskets for shoes by the door)?

- Does each family member have his or her own personal space, including a private place to be alone and an area designated for his or her belongings?

- Is there a system for organizing and managing essential information (e.g., telephone messages, appointments, receipts, invitations, communications between family members)?

- Are the items needed to complete tasks or activities accessible (e.g., the cleaning supplies for chores are in one particular cabinet, the pencils and paper for homework or telephone messages are kept in the kitchen)?

- Are areas designated for particular kinds of activities (e.g., mealtimes, homework, entertaining friends) and is there sufficient space allotted for those activities?

- Are the furnishings arranged to facilitate parental supervision as appropriate (e.g., the play area is close to the kitchen, the bedroom doors are open when the children have friends visiting, the computer and telephone are accessible to the entire family)?

- Have safety issues (e.g., childproofing, keeping doors locked) been considered and addressed?

- Is the home organized to minimize distractions (e.g., the homework station is away from the telephone and front door, the television is turned off during conversations) that might interfere with the activities of the family members?

- Are items that are not used frequently stored out of the way and unnecessary clutter disposed of regularly (e.g., seasonal clothing is stored in the attic, seldom used toys are boxed way)?

- Are items that are off limits or restricted in terms of accessibility locked away, out of reach, or clearly designated as unavailable (e.g., tools, cleaning chemicals, cosmetics, after-dinner treats)?

Structuring our homes to address these kinds of issues provides visual reminders of the expectations and reduces the need to hassle over the same issues over and over (e.g., "Why are there crumbs in the couch?" "Who left shoes in the kitchen?" "Why are you watching television instead of doing your homework?").

Time

Managing time refers to the way in which we structure our families' typical schedules and routines and establish time limits for activities. How we use our time may be fixed or flexible, depending on our families' values and needs. Many children and families, however, prefer some degree of predictability. The comfort of knowing when a routine is going to happen can provide stability for our families and allow us to focus on what we are currently doing and prepare for the next activity. Organizing time may also help us be more productive and efficient, which may be especially important given how many activities are woven into our families' busy schedules.

One way in which we deal with time is to have a schedule of activities for our families, usually structured around work or school, mealtimes, and curfews and/or bedtimes. Having consistency in our schedule helps us to organize our day, ensure that everyone in our family is getting adequate nutrition and rest, and get our family members where they need to be when they need to be there. For example, a typical day for a family with young children might include consistent meal and snack times, naps, story time, play dates, outside playtime, and preschool activities. A family with older children may have more flexible schedules orchestrated around sports and other after-school activities, homework, and the time the children spend hanging out with their friends.

In addition to our schedule, we may establish other timelines to keep our lives manageable. This means determining how long or how often activities will occur in our homes. For example, we might

- Say the family must eat together a certain number of times per week

- Limit how many extracurricular activities our children participate in

- Clarify how much television and computer time is allowable

- Restrict sleepovers or dinner guests to certain days of the week

Obviously, there are times when such limits should be ignored for the purpose of family fun (e.g., sleeping in on weekends, delaying lunch so there is more time to swim in the pool, staying out late to see fireworks). As a general rule, however, having time limits can help us avoid overscheduling, which can place stress on a family, and provide greater consistency in expectations for all family members.

A final feature of organizing our time is for us to establish or change routines. Routines are predictable sequences of activity; they are how we do what we do. Most people have routines for getting ready in the morning, preparing meals, completing housework or homework, returning home from school or work, going to bed at night, and other typical daily activities. Effective routines can help us to organize and use our time more efficiently, as well as build upon our household expectations. Routines can also be problematic. For example, if one parent's routine is to read the mail and relax in front of the television immediately upon returning home in the evening, that routine may not meet the needs of his or her young children who have been looking forward to seeing their parent all day.

Routines may be especially important when multiple family members are trying to get things done all at once. Here is an example of a routine a family might establish for getting ready in the morning:

Becka, the mother, and Andy, a preschooler, bathe the night before, leaving the shower free to the rest of the family the next morning. Jenny, whose school starts earliest, showers first and then does her make-up and hair in her bedroom. Mark, the father, jogs in the morning, so Luke showers next. He is out of the shower by the time Mark gets back, so Mark has plenty of time to shave and shower before going to work. Becka waits to wake Andy up until the rest of the family is ready for breakfast so that Andy does not interfere with the routine by demanding a lot of attention or assistance. Becka sets out cereal, muffins, and whatever other breakfast choices are available and prepares Andy's breakfast. Jenny and Luke prepare their own food and watch Andy while Becka gets ready for the day. Everyone clears his or her own dishes and puts them in the dishwasher. Once breakfast has been eaten, everyone makes sure that all of the materials he or she needs for the day are ready by the front door.

The way in which we choose to arrange our household will vary based on preferences of our individual families. For example, if a family desires a lot of peace and quiet, they might limit television time and discourage uninvited guests. If a family finds family unity important, they might schedule frequent time together such as during weekend activities and meals. If a family wants to focus on maintaining order, they might organize their space more productively and establish a more consistent daily schedule. Regardless of the changes we choose to make, many problems can be avoided when we attend carefully to the structure and routines of our households.

Activity: Structuring the Home

How can you organize your space to support your family expectations (encourage positive behavior and minimize problems)?

_____

_____

_____

How can you organize your time to support your family expectations?

Overall schedule: _____

_____

_____

Timelines:_____

_____

_____

Daily routines: _____

_____

_____

Responding to Behavior

In addition to arranging our households in ways that tend to prevent problems from occurring, a powerful way for us to help our family members meet the established expectations is to make sure we respond to behavior in ways that encourage adherence to rules and discourage rule breaking. When we give clear, consistent consequences, family members begin to understand that following rules is a choice and that they can control the positive and negative outcomes of their behavior. We can apply to the entire family the same approaches to rewarding positive behavior and deterring problem behavior that were described in Chapter 5 and that have been drawn from schoolwide approaches.

Encouraging Family Members to Follow Expectations

Providing positive feedback to family members is essential to support and encourage family expectations. Specifically, this means acknowledging and rewarding family members when they follow household rules. Because it is generally not second nature for people to focus on appropriate behavior (historically there has been more emphasis on disciplining misbehavior rather than encouraging positive behavior), it can be helpful for families to create a plan for encouraging appropriate behavior. Our families may need to discuss specifically how to encourage and support each other and to continually focus on the positive contributions that every family member makes. Three ways we may use to encourage our families to follow the rules are 1) providing praise and feedback for behavior, 2) linking privileges to appropriate behavior, and 3) working rewards into the daily routine.

Providing praise simply means that we make sure we acknowledge the behavior aligned with our expectations. For example, everyone in a family can get in the habit of thanking each other or praising specific acts, such as helping to do the household chores or treating the other family members kindly (e.g., "Thanks for the dinner," "Your bedroom looks so clean and fantastic," "I know you were angry at me, but you kept your temper and did not yell"). The primary goal of praising is for positive behavior to be noticed and commented on—at least as often, if not more frequently, than misbehavior is corrected.

Privileges include anything we provide beyond what is required to feed, clothe, and shelter our families. Some common privileges are a monetary allowance; access to the television and computer; the availability of transportation; special activities, toys, and treats; and being excused from doing chores. Many families give their children a monetary allowance for doing chores, but often we forget that many of the privileges we provide do not need to be given automatically. To encourage family expectations, many—if not all—of these privileges should be linked to positive behavior. Privileges should be earned for following family rules and withheld for violations. We can determine how we will respond to requests for special privileges by doing a quick review of our children's recent behavior. Something as simple as determining whether to say yes or no to a privilege based on children's current behavior can teach children that their behavior determines their rewards.

We can also work rewards into our families' daily routines. For example, we might offer a dessert only after family members have finished dinner, let our children watch television in the morning if they get ready quickly and have time before leaving for school, or go out to a movie together if everyone pitches in to complete a project or followed all of the rules that week. Rewards that are part of daily routines should pertain to every member of the family—including parents.

Discouraging Rule Breaking

In order to reinforce our expectations for our families, we also need to provide feedback and consequences when the house rules are broken. This means that either family members do not receive the rewards (e.g., allowance, privileges) they are accustomed to or that the behavior results in consequences that are likely to deter such behavior in the future. The consequences should be preestablished, logical, and natural (as described in Chapter 5), and—to the greatest extent possible—agreed upon by the entire family. Being clear and reasonable about consequences, and ensuring that everyone in the family understands them, tends to avoid situations where family members engage in power struggles and to negate the bad feelings that often come with arbitrary punishment. Some examples of consequences include the following:

- For leaving the house without permission or for breaking curfew, family members are restricted to staying within the house for a reasonable length of time.

- For whining, arguing, or otherwise disrupting family life, family members will have a time-out in their bedroom until they are willing to discuss the given situation calmly or accept consequences as appropriate.

- For fighting, family members must be separated until they calm down, their differences must be resolved, and a plan must be made in case the situation arises again.

As mentioned in Chapter 5, natural and logical consequences also means we must avoid bailing our children out if their behavior results in undesirable consequences (e.g., leaving them to pay off their own cellular telephone charges, not replacing their toys if they damage them).

Consequences (both positive and negative) must be used consistently in order to improve behavior. Therefore, consequences must be chosen with care and should be respectful and feasible for all family members. Prior to establishing consequences, we should determine whether the consequences fit with our families' expectations and whether the consequences are a reasonable reaction in terms of their length or intensity when compared to the behavior. We should also consider the impact of the consequences on the family members who are not misbehaving. For example, Andreya, a teenager, misses curfew on a school night and therefore loses the privilege to use the family car. By imposing this restriction, other family members (e.g., her parents) may have to cancel their own plans in order to provide transportation for the family. In this case, the consequences are unduly inconvenient for everyone. Andreya's parents may decide that it would be better to have her continue transporting her younger siblings but not be able to drive with her friends. Consequences must fit with a family's needs and situations. Table 7 provides further examples of rewards and consequences that we might establish based on our house rules.

Table 7. Examples of rewards and consequences

Family expectations	Rewards	Consequences
Be kind and respectful to others (e.g., listen when others talk, communicate without using physical actions, speak in a calm voice, use polite words).	Offer to let the children do a fun activity quietly (e.g., go swimming, read a book) and only let the children who respond to your offer participate. Praise good manners (e.g., listening, saying "please" and "thank you"). Encourage the children to talk about their feelings appropriately (e.g., telling someone when they are angry rather than shouting).	Give one warning for yelling, whining, or making threats and insults, then ask the children to go to their bedrooms until they can be nice and remind them to express their feelings respectfully. Separate the children immediately when they hurt each other. Make them discuss the problem, and take away privileges as needed.
Take responsibility for yourself, your actions, and your things (e.g., clean up your messes, do the chores assigned to you).	Provide a monetary allowance at the end of each week if the children have completed all of their assigned chores. Praise the children for helping to do unassigned chores around the house, and provide a bonus for special jobs. Pick a family project to do each weekend and follow the completion of the project with an outing (e.g., going out for ice cream). Let the children go play with their friends after they have finished their chores.	Withhold or reduce allowance when the children do not complete their chores. Refuse to allow the children to take part in a special event (e.g., visiting a friend) if they have not been helpful around the house.

Activity: Responding to Behavior

For each of the family expectations, answer how you will 1) reward behavior to encourage the following of a given rule (e.g., provide praise, privileges) and 2) provide a consequence to discourage violations of the rule (i.e., natural and logical consequences).

Family expectations	Rewards	Consequences

PROBLEM-SOLVING DIFFICULT SITUATIONS AND ROUTINES

Even generally well-organized and positive families experience periodic problems with certain situations or routines. Another component of PBS is for us to apply the same problem-solving process described in Section II to consider why certain circumstances may be particularly difficult for our entire families. When problems for our whole families arise, we can use the PBS process to sort the problems out and determine how to address them. We can take the following steps:

- Define the specific behaviors of concern and broader goals we are working toward.

- Gather information to better understand the circumstances and outcomes contributing to the problem behavior.

- Create and implement strategies for preventing problems, replacing behavior, and managing consequences more effectively.

- Monitor and evaluate the changes we experience.

The following chapter segments describe and illustrate how this problem-solving process can be used to resolve problems within particular family situations or routines.

Establishing Goals

If we are having problems with particular situations or routines, it is important for us to consider what behaviors we want to occur—or how we want to function as a family—during those times, what behaviors are currently happening, and what specific circumstances and behaviors we might want to change. For example, the Williamsons, a family of two adults and four children, might have pleasant mealtimes and a wonderful tradition of a weekly family night with games, outings, movies, or other activities. The Williamsons, however, might also face problems with transitions between home and school or work in which everyone is stressed out and behaving badly (e.g., frequently arguing with each other). Therefore, the Williamsons' family goal would be to improve those transitions and reduce the time spent arguing with each other so that transition times become as pleasant as the family nights.

Gathering Information

Once we have identified our goals, we can employ the same strategies described in Chapter 4 to gather and analyze information to better understand why behavior problems occur in certain situations. We can pay close attention during those times (e.g., watching for patterns, talking to each other about what is happening and why, and, if necessary, recording the behaviors and circumstances) in an effort to identify the reasons for problems. Using the information we find, we can ask ourselves questions about the situations:

- What might be contributing to our family's best and worst times?

- What outcomes or results might be perpetuating those patterns?

By looking carefully and objectively at different circumstances or routines, we can often identify patterns. Returning to the story of the Williamson family, mealtimes and family nights might be pleasant situations because there are consistent expectations for those times, the rewards used are part of the activities themselves (e.g., positive family interactions, good food), and the atmosphere is in general more relaxed. In contrast, transition times may be chaotic and rushed (e.g., family members busily going from one place to the next, trying to find what they need, competing for the bathroom and use of the car). The Williamsons might discover that during transitions the parents tend to give a greater amount of attention to problem behavior (e.g., nagging the children to hurry up) than to positive behavior or address behavior unproductively (e.g., using insults, sarcasm, or threats). Through this process of recognizing patterns, the Williamsons can discover that arguing delays unpleasant activities and/or gains greater amounts of help from others. Identifying patterns like these can be very useful when we try to address our problem situations.

Developing a Plan

Using this understanding about what is affecting our families' behavior during particular times, it is possible to make changes to prevent or minimize problems, replace unpleasant interactions with positive behaviors, and manage the consequences to encourage those new behaviors.

Preventing Problems

It may be possible for us to change our families' surroundings or routines to minimize conflict and help situations go more smoothly during difficult transitions. For example, the Williamsons might reorganize entry areas to facilitate smoother transitions (e.g., identifying specific places for book bags, wallets, purses, shoes, and so forth). They can lay out clothes, prepare lunches (or lunch money), plan meals, adjust bath times, make other preparations the night before, or wake up earlier so that all family members have more time in the morning. Other things may be done to allow the Williamsons to minimize distractions (e.g., not answer the telephone, keep the television turned off) during their difficult times, establish more consistent routines for transition periods, and communicate with the entire family each individual's needs (see the Structuring Our Home segment of this chapter for more examples of this). These things might be very helpful for making transition times easier and more pleasant for the Williamson family.

Replacing Behavior

We may come to recognize that our family has fallen into patterns of unpleasant or unproductive behavior, particularly during stressful periods. For example, the Williamson family might use their household rules as a starting point for addressing their behavior during transitions. It may be necessary for the family to more clearly define their expectations for behavior during the transition periods (e.g., chore responsibilities are written down and posted clearly) and possibly encourage some new skills in order to function better as a family. The Williamsons may need to use some time and stress management skills (e.g., prioritizing and scheduling, taking deep breaths to alleviate anxiety) and to communicate more effectively with each other, (e.g., "I'm feeling rushed; I need more time").

Managing Consequences

In order to replace problem behavior with positive alternatives, the new behaviors must be rewarded and the inappropriate behavior patterns no longer encouraged. In difficult situations we may need to consider which behaviors get most of our attention—good or bad—or other beneficial outcomes and whether problem behavior (e.g., arguing, delaying chores) causes family members to avoid disagreeable activities. If the negative behavior is inadvertently being rewarded, these patterns of response should be adjusted.

Since the Williamson family's transitions are particularly difficult, the parents might decide to use special rewards during those times. The Williamsons want to praise any positive behavior that occurs in transition times. The parents could make treats like watching television or doing fun activities available only after family members have completed their chores or routines. The parents may also negotiate responsibilities for a larger reward (e.g., if the children get themselves ready to leave the house and are ready on time four out of five days during the week, the parents will treat them to ice cream on the way home from school on Friday). The Williamsons may also want to use logical or natural consequences to respond to problem behavior (e.g., ignoring behaviors that interfere with positive transitions, providing quickly made cold breakfasts instead of time-intensive hot breakfasts on the mornings their children delay getting ready for school).

Examples of problem solving for difficult family routines (e.g., mealtimes, greeting people outside the family, and playing without parental supervision) are included in Appendix C at the end of this book.

Activity: Problem-Solving Situations and Routines

Situations: _____

What are the goals for your family (e.g., changes desired, behaviors of concern) during your family's difficult situation?

_____

_____

What patterns might be contributing to your behavior as a family during this routine?

The circumstances associated with your best and worst times:

_____

_____

The outcomes causing the patterns to continue:

_____

_____

Given your understanding about the patterns surrounding problem routines, what strategies might you put in place to

Prevent problems?

_____

_____

_____

Replace behavior?

_____

_____

_____

Manage consequences?

_____

_____

_____

As with our plans for improving our children's behavior, we also need to monitor the results of the strategies for our families as a whole. To be consistent and effective, we need a way to determine if we are achieving our families' visions and household expectations. For many families, this may be best done jointly by all family members (e.g., by going over goals each morning at breakfast and then reviewing performance at bedtime, by having weekly family meetings where events and behavior are discussed). PBS in families should be seen as a continual process in which our families assess how they are responding to problem behavior and problem-solve difficult situations as the need arises.

SUMMARY

PBS is a framework and a process that can be used to enhance our family lives, as well as to improve the behavior of our individual children experiencing behavior difficulties. We can incorporate the principles of PBS into our homes by determining our family goals, paying attention to the circumstances that affect the behavior of our family members, and making changes in our responses to encourage positive behavior and discourage problem behavior. If we incorporate PBS into our daily lives and ongoing decision making, we can create more enjoyable and satisfying home lives.

Before Moving On

Do you have a vision and clearly defined expectations for your family?

Have you organized your household space and time in a way that supports the kinds of interactions you desire as a family?

Do you have consistent ways of encouraging positive behavior (e.g., following the rules) and discouraging negative behavior (e.g., breaking the rules)?

Have you looked closely at any problem routines for your family and made changes to improve them?

CHAPTER 11

Making Positive Behavior Support Work for Everyone

PBS, whether used to address the behavior of individual children or to improve family life in general, can be extremely successful. The process helps to resolve behavior problems and improve lives by providing a flexible approach that can be used in a variety of situations and adapted to fit the needs of different individuals and environments. In order for PBS to be effective, however, it must be used with some degree of precision and consistency, which is not always easy. For us to faithfully apply PBS principles with our children and families, we must be willing to look beyond our children's problem behavior to consider our own behavior and interactions with our children. This chapter discusses three critical issues in making PBS work: 1) examining and changing our own behavior, 2) teaching our children how to manage their behavior, and 3) helping all the family members and others involved (e.g., teachers, extended family, baby sitters) work together to improve behavior. This chapter concludes with a brief summary of what we have learned about parenting with PBS throughout this book.

ADDRESSING OUR OWN BEHAVIOR

Changing our children's behavior typically requires that we also change our own behavior, specifically how we observe, approach, and respond to difficult situations. One reason why parenting is so difficult is because we must be willing to realistically assess our performance and think about how our behaviors and interactions may be contributing to our children's problems and conflicts with others. We need to consider the input and advice of other people and accept new ideas that might benefit our children and families. We must also be able to look objectively at stressful and frustrating situations in order to better gain an understanding of what behaviors are occurring and why, and then we must be prepared to manage and control our own behavior so we can be patient, mature, and consistent even when the circumstances are difficult. We might ask ourselves the following questions when evaluating our own behavior:

- "Do we model the behaviors we want our children to use, or do we speak or act in ways that contradict out stated expectations?"

- "Are we consistent with our expectations and follow through with consequences, or do we resort to idle threats and knee-jerk reactions?"

- "Are we encouraging our children to be self-sufficient, or are we protecting our children from natural consequences and creating unnecessary dependencies?"

Based on the answers to these questions, we will probably identify areas in which our performance is very strong and consistent and other areas where we would like our behavior to change. For example, Vanessa, a single parent of three grade-school children, might discover that although most of the time she is loving, open, and fair with her children, she also has a tendency to become angry or frustrated with them—yelling, threatening, and even grabbing them. In certain situations, Vanessa reacts impulsively and in ways that are not particularly beneficial or effective in the long term.

We can use the principles of PBS described in this book to look closely at our own behavior, determine when we are most and least effective at influencing our children's behavior, and consider the circumstances that contribute to our effectiveness. By analyzing our own behavior, the surrounding circumstances, and our children's reactions to our behavior, we may come to realize the reasons for our reactions to our children and use this understanding to create a plan for changing or modifying our own behavior.

Upon reflection, Vanessa may see that she is more inclined to become angry and frustrated at her children when she is stressed by an increase in demands at work or home. When the family's daily schedule gets compressed or her list of things to do gets too long, Vanessa finds herself yelling, threatening, or grabbing her children when they misbehave. If she reacts this way, her children tend to stop their behaviors immediately and leave Vanessa alone, giving her a moment's peace—all of which only provides her with a quick fix and may actually strengthen her negative patterns of behavior. As Vanessa considers the patterns, she may also come to realize that she is less likely to become upset with her children when she makes a point of spending some time relaxing by herself each day.

Armed with this type of awareness, we can make changes to prevent or minimize the circumstances that set the stage our unwanted behavior. We can replace our automatic reactions with more positive, purposeful, and workable strategies and then reward ourselves when we have successful interactions. For example, Vanessa might decide that she needs to set aside some special time for herself so that she can relax after a difficult day at work, spend some time thinking, reflect on her interactions with her children, and plan her next day's schedule. She could use this time to further analyze what prompts her reactions to her children's behavior and consider ways she could avoid negative patterns in the future. If particular situations or behaviors of her children tend to irritate or upset her, Vanessa could determine what these behaviors are and how she might be able to minimize their effect (e.g., responding to her children's teasing of each other before the teasing escalates into a fight, consistently rewarding her children for being kind to each other).

Vanessa also may need to monitor herself so that she can recognize when she needs to relax and regain composure during stressful circumstances. She might think about what she can say or do in these situations so that she can have a situation script to follow. For example, she might tell her children, "I am really stressed out right now and I do not want to take it out on you. Can I have a few minutes to myself?" and then go to a room away from the children for a few minutes.

We may benefit from using some internal dialogue in order to redirect our own behavior, such as "What behavior am I modeling for my children right now?" Once we have a plan to adjust our behavior, we need to regularly evaluate how well our strategies are working. When we find we are handling difficult circumstances appropriately, we need to acknowledge our actions and maybe even reward ourselves (e.g., have a night off from preparing dinner by ordering take-out).

When we make mistakes and mishandle situations with our children's behavior, which will occasionally happen, we need to make an effort to repair the situation (e.g., apologize to our children), consider how our actions were inappropriate and what contributed to the problem, decide how we could react to the situation the next time it occurs, and move on. We are not perfect, and parenting is not an exact science. It is important for us to use our mistakes by treating them as valuable learning experiences and making adjustments to better support our behavior and needs. We can also act as models, showing our children how to use problem-solving skills and teaching our children how to repair an action they regret doing. Through the PBS process, we are continually striving to be proud of ourselves and our role as parents, purposefully and positively reacting to and interacting with our children.

HELPING CHILDREN MANAGE THEIR OWN BEHAVIOR

We want our children to grow up to become many things: happy, healthy, capable, responsible, productive, and independent. When our children are young, we give them everything they need and provide tight boundaries for their behavior. When our children are babies, we respond quickly when our children cry, childproof our homes, watch our children carefully, and are extremely particular about who cares for our children. As our children grow, we are no longer able to provide that kind of supervision and guidance—nor do we want to. Our children begin to visit friends' homes without supervision, look to other adults for direction, and make their own daily decisions. Over time, we come to realize that many of the actions and interactions influencing our children's behavior are outside of our control (e.g., the way in which our children interact with their friends). We may not even be aware of some of the events that happen to our children and affect their behavior. Even if we share our children's experiences, we may have little influence on our children's behavior when compared with the influence of our children's peers.

As children become more independent, it is important that they learn to regulate their own behavior and make sensible decisions. We cannot and should not try to orchestrate every situation that affects our children; instead, we must hope that our children have internalized the values and skills we have taught them and will behave accordingly.

The question we should ask ourselves is, "How can we help our children learn to make good decisions and demonstrate self-discipline?" Preparing our children to care for themselves and regulate their own behavior does not happen immediately or without effort. Instead, it is best achieved when we guide and gradually empower (i.e., teach) our children, and then—as our children become more capable and self-sufficient—reduce our involvement and influence.

There are a number of useful books and training programs on the topic of empowering children (see the Parenting Resources section of the Bibliography at the end of the book). PBS offers us some guidance in achieving two primary goals with our children:

1. Developing personal values that children can use to guide how they will behave in different situations

2. Teaching children the principles of PBS so that they can understand and manage their own behavior

Developing Values

Our primary goal as parents is to impart personal values that are essential to our families and that our children can use to guide and evaluate their own actions (e.g., see the Establishing a Family Vision and Expectations segment of Chapter 10). These values will vary between families and individuals but may include broad concepts such as integrity, respect, kindness, appreciation, sensitivity, risk taking, self-restraint, or creativity. It is important for us to clarify our families' values and deliberately teach our children how to behave in accordance with those values. By doing so, our values will become a basic guide that our children can apply to any situation and use to make appropriate decisions. Using these values as a foundation, our children can learn to recognize and build on their own personal strengths and adjust their behavior when it does not conform to these ideals (i.e., when they do something wrong). They can also learn to look critically at their own behavior and evaluate if the behavior is acceptable, just as we may have done for them over the years.

Teaching values begins with us making sure our children understand what it means to adhere to these values. For example, we might define the term *kindness* in relation to how people interact physically (e.g., touching others gently, respecting personal space, offering assistance) or interact socially (e.g., providing compliments or reassurances, demonstrating respect for individual differences). We can point out and provide examples of behaviors that align with and violate this value and ask our children questions that will help them learn how to decide for themselves (e.g., "If this situation happened to you, how would you be kind?"). Once our children understand the values expected of them, we can guide them to evaluate and adjust their behavior in daily interactions.

Teaching Positive Behavior Support Principles

In addition to teaching basic values, we can also help our children apply the basic principles of behavior presented in this book to their own behavior. PBS does not have to be a secret code practiced exclusively by us; we can teach our children to use the strategies and ideas that underlie the PBS process for themselves. Our children can learn that all behaviors have a purpose and that they can use this knowledge to change their own behavior. We can encourage our children to ask themselves questions like, "What was going on when I behaved that way?" "How did I react when in that circumstance?" "Was there a better way I could have reacted?" "What did I get because of the way I behaved?" "What did I avoid?"

With this knowledge, our children can develop their own behavior plans. They can prevent problems from occurring by changing the circumstances that provoke problems with their behavior, learning new ways to meet their needs, and regulating the results of their behavior. Table 8 describes the internal dialogue a child might use as he or she observes his or her own behavior, tries to understand why the behavior is occurring, and creates a plan for the next time this situation occurs. Teaching our children the skills they need to monitor and change their own behavior is essential because it allows them to gain independence and improve their self-control, rather than always being dependent on other people (e.g., their parents) for guidance and approval. Shifting this responsibility away from us and toward our children is not easy, and it requires that we take a more facilitative than directive posture. In essence, that means that we step back from being involved in certain situations and guide our children through them instead—becoming our children's coaches, cheerleaders, and collaborators. Instead of telling our children what to do, we ask questions or provide subtle prompts that help our children find answers to problems on their own. Instead of solving our children's problems for them or immediately doling out consequences, we allow our children to make their own choices and be responsible for the outcomes of their behavior. We do not tell our children how to act or think but instead teach our children how to assess the circumstances and adjust their behavior accordingly. In order to do this successfully, we have to really listen and pay attention to our children and try to understand what they experience.

Table 8.   Examples of internal dialogue

What happened?	"I yelled at my mother when she did not come to help me with my homework right away."
Why did it happen?	"When I have to wait for assistance, I get mad and sometimes yell. Then I do not get any help and cannot finish my work."
What can I do?	"I can start my homework earlier when I have more time, and then I can take breaks if I get frustrated. If I am doing something that is hard for me, I can let my mother know that I will probably need help by remaining calm and asking nicely. If I do not yell the next time I do homework, I will point this out to my mother and play my favorite video game when I am finished as a self-reward."

WORKING TOGETHER TO IMPROVE BEHAVIOR

One of the most important requirements—and often one of the greatest frustrations—to implementing PBS is getting all our family members and all other people involved in our children's care to agree and commit to the goals and strategies of the behavior support plans. As individuals, we may be trying to make positive changes in our children's behavior, but we are probably not the only people who can and will effect the outcomes of the plans. We may need to coordinate with our spouses, friends, and extended family; our children's peers, teachers, and child care providers; and other adults who care for and interact with our children.

A cohesive approach to parenting and discipline is important in general, but it is often absolutely essential when our children are experiencing behavior problems or our families are having difficulty. Getting so many people to work together, however, is not easy, especially when we factor in the challenges that come with parenting children with difficult behavior while at the same time attending to all the other needs of our families. This may be particularly true today given the frequency of complex family situations (e.g., shared custody, blended families), the variety of extracurricular activities in which children often participate, and the generally high pressure of family life.

There are a number of reasons why some people may resist working together. First, we all have unique approaches to given situations, with different perspectives, assumptions, and parenting styles (e.g., some parents are more permissive, some parents are more firm). We may become so wedded to our own ideas or determined to be right that we are unwilling to consider anyone else's opinion. We might be so busy trying to complete our own daily tasks that we do not realize we are making important decisions without first consulting others. There could also be problems in our interpersonal relationships, and how those problems are addressed can greatly affect our children's behavior (e.g., one parent releases the children from a restriction because he or she is irritated with the other parent's recent behavior toward the children).

We have to acknowledge that there may be challenges when people work together, but there are also many important benefits when we can arrange this successfully. The following things are possible when we enlist the aid and support of people who are involved in our children's and families' lives:

- We can hear other people's perspectives and therefore learn more about our children and what affects their behavior.

- We are better able to create plans that work for our children, fit our families' lives, and achieve our goals.

- We are more committed to our goals and therefore are better able to use strategies consistently and effectively.

- We are able to learn and grow along with the other people involved in the process, people who also help us celebrate successes and support us when difficulties arise.

Given the challenges and potential benefits of working together, we may wonder how we can make this collaboration work? How can we support our children's teachers when we do not always agree with the teachers' approaches? How can we confront a grandparent whose parenting style undermines our efforts? How do we work with a parenting partner to present a unified front to our children? Collaboration requires that everyone work together toward a single common goal. Everyone involved must take part in creating a unified vision, maintaining a consistent approach, and sharing the responsibility to put the behavior strategies into action. There are a number of resources available on the topic of collaboration (see Parenting Resources section in the Bibliography); however, the next sections in this chapter provide a few important tips that can help us work together toward using PBS successfully.

Involve the Right People

There may be a number of people who could make or break behavior plans for our children. We need to make an effort to include those other individuals who know our children well, interact with our children regularly, and are responsible for our children's education and care. For children with more complex needs (e.g., those who have disabilities or are having problems at school or in the community), children with particularly challenging behavior, or children who depend on many types of support and services, successfully using the PBS process may require asking even more individuals to help. All of the people involved in the process should be included from the start and at all critical points in the PBS process (e.g., when designing the plan).

Acknowledge Differences

When trying to work with other people, we need to be aware of and respect the inevitable differences in perspectives. Some people involved in our children's or families' lives might perceive themselves as traditional in terms of the expectations of our children's behavior while other people may view those expectations as overly rigid or permissive. The objective of working together should be to get a general consensus on principles without stifling individual differences because those differences might ultimately benefit our children. It is not necessary for everyone to implement strategies in exactly the same way; variability across people and places can be helpful to the process provided that everyone maintains some consistency on basic principles, as well as shared goals, plans, and responsibilities.

Communicate Consistently

To work together, we must communicate with one another. This means setting aside enough time to talk with (or write to) each other. For example, we may find the best time to talk to each other is after our children go to bed at night or right before they get up in the morning. We may want to schedule family meetings that include extended family members or close friends, or try to communicate with a child's teacher via e-mail. When we do communicate about the PBS process, it is important that we be open and focused, sharing with candor our goals, observations, ideas, and needs.

Solve Problems Together

Given our differences in perspectives, the many demands we may have on our time, and the challenges in dealing with problem behavior, conflict between individuals is probably inevitable. We therefore need to find a way to make decisions (especially big decisions) concerning the process and our children and solve problems together. It may be helpful to create in advance rules of interaction that can help deal with conflict effectively. For example, we might decide that we will only disagree in private (out of sight or sound of our children), that we will focus on solving problems rather than finding blame, and that we will continue to communicate until we have resolution. We may have to negotiate compromises or even yield completely to one another at times to resolve problems and keep the lines of communication open.

Use Positive Behavior Support Principles in Interactions

We can use the principles of PBS described in this book to improve our interactions with one another and facilitate collaboration. For example, rather than jumping to conclusions about another person's motives, we can work to observe that person's behavior and circumstances and communicate openly with him or her in order to better understand why he or she is behaving in that particular way. We may be able to prevent future conflicts with our spouses and between other adults by monitoring how, when, and where we broach unpleasant topics. We also are more likely to work together effectively if we are supportive and encouraging, thanking each other for his or her efforts rather than criticizing mistakes.

When we come together to use PBS, agree on common goals, and follow some basic guidelines, the solutions can be quite powerful. A unified solution is almost always greater than a solution generated by any individual.

SUMMARY

Although PBS has been used most extensively in schools and community programs, it was neither designed nor intended for use exclusively by professionals. The basic principles of behavior on which PBS is based are applicable for everyone. Because of the essential role we assume in guiding and supporting our children, we are the people most likely to need and benefit from this approach, and we are capable of doing this effectively and well. Through PBS, we can develop a better understanding of why our children use inappropriate behavior and address our children's behavior through prevention, teaching, and management of consequences.

In summary, PBS provides certain basic lessons we can use in our daily lives. We can

- *Understand behavior:* By stepping back, remaining open to other viewpoints, and looking for patterns in daily interactions, we can come to understand the purposes behavior serves and the circumstances that encourage it (what, where, when, who, and why).

- *Be proactive:* Rather than waiting for problems to occur, we can anticipate and prevent them through the ways we structure our homes, lives, and living situations.

- *Teach skills:* We can view behavior problems simply as our children's inappropriate ways of dealing with their circumstances and meeting their needs. We can therefore help our children develop new and better ways of achieving those goals.

- *React purposefully:* Knowing that the way we respond to our children and others influences our children's behavior, whether our actions are intentional or not, we can deliberately behave in ways that encourage positive behavior, instead of perpetuating problems.

PBS provides these foundations and offers a flexible framework by which we can determine what behaviors we want our children to use and how to encourage behavior changes to happen. The process provides a general standard by which we can make reasonable decisions and select from among the wide array of options suggested by our families and friends; by health care providers and teachers, and by the media. PBS gives us a process for solving our own problems with our children, in our homes, and in our lives—especially as time passes, children grow and develop, and new circumstances arise. PBS provides us with the right questions so we can generate the right solutions.

Bibliography

POSITIVE BEHAVIOR SUPPORT

Bambara, L.M., & Kern, L. (2005). *Individualized supports for students with problem behaviors: Designing positive behavior support plans.* New York: The Guilford Press.

Boettcher, M., Koegel, R.L., McNerney, E.K., & Koegel, L.K. (2003). A family-centered prevention approach to PBS in a time of crisis. *Journal of Positive Behavior Interventions, 5,* 55–60.

Buschbacher, P., Fox, L., & Clarke, S. (2004). Recapturing desired family routines: A parent–professional behavioral collaboration. *Research and Practice for Persons with Severe Disabilities, 29,* 25–39.

Carr, E.G., Dunlap, G., Horner, R.H., Koegel, R.L., Turnbull, A., Sailor, W., et al. (2002). Positive behavior support: Evolution of an applied science. *Journal of Positive Behavior Interventions, 4,* 4–16.

Carr, E.G., Levin, L., McConnachie, G., Carlson, J.I., Kemp, D.C., & Smith, C.E. (1994). *Communication-based intervention for problem behavior: A user's guide for producing positive change.* Baltimore: Paul H. Brookes Publishing Co.

Crone, D.A., & Horner, R.H. (2003). *Building positive behavior support in schools: Functional behavioral assessment.* New York: The Guilford Press.

Dunlap, G., Fox., L., & Vaughn, B.J. (2003). Families, problem behavior, and positive behavior support. *TASH Connections, 29,* 28–31.

Dunlap, G., Newton, J.S., Fox, L., Benito, N., & Vaughn, B. (2001). Family involvement in functional assessment and positive behavior support. *Focus on Autism and Other Developmental Disabilities, 16,* 215–221.

Fox, L., Dunlap, G., & Cushing, L. (2002). Early intervention, positive behavior support, and transition to school. *Journal of Emotional and Behavioral Disorders, 10,* 149–157.

Fox, L., Vaughn, B.J., Wyatte, M.L., & Dunlap, G. (2002). "We can't expect other people to understand:" Family perspectives on problem behavior. *Exceptional Children, 68,* 437–450.

Hieneman, M., & Dunlap, G. (1999). Issues and challenges in implementing community-based behavioral support for two boys with severe behavioral difficulties. In J.R. Scotti & L.H. Meyer (Eds.), *Behavioral intervention: Principles, models, and practices* (pp. 363–384). Baltimore: Paul H. Brookes Publishing Co.

Hieneman, M., & Dunlap, G. (2000). Factors affecting the outcomes of community-based behavioral support: Identification and description of factor categories. *Journal of Positive Behavior Interventions, 2,* 161–169.

Hieneman, M., Nolan, M., Presley, J., DeTuro, L., Roberson, W., & Dunlap, G. (1999). *Facilitator's guide: Positive behavioral support.* Tallahassee: Florida Department of Education, Bureau of Instructional Support and Community Services.

Holburn, S., & Vietze, P. (Eds.). (2002). *Person-centered planning: Research, practice, and future directions.* Baltimore: Paul H. Brookes Publishing Co.

Horner, R.H., Dunlap, G., Koegel, R.L., Carr, E.G., Sailor, W., Anderson, J., et al. (1990). Toward a technology of "nonaversive" behavioral support. *Journal of The Association for Persons with Severe Handicaps, 15,* 125–132.

Jackson, L., & Panyan, M.V. (2001). *Positive behavioral support in the classroom: Principles and practices.* Baltimore: Paul H. Brookes Publishing Co.

Knoster, T.P. (2000). Practical application of functional behavioral assessment in schools. *Journal of The Association for Persons with Severe Handicaps, 25,* 201–211.

Koegel, L.K., Koegel, R.L., & Dunlap, G. (Eds.). (1996). *Positive behavioral support: Including people with difficult behavior in the community.* Baltimore: Paul H. Brookes Publishing Co.

Lewis, T.J., Sugai, G., & Garrison-Harrell, T. (1999). Effective behavior support: Designing setting-specific interventions. *Effective School Practices, 17,* 38–46.

Lucyshyn, J.M., Dunlap, G., & Albin, R.W. (Eds.). (2002). *Families and positive behavior support: Addressing problem behavior in family contexts.* Baltimore: Paul H. Brookes Publishing Co.

Marshall, J.K., & Mirenda, P. (2002). Parent–professional collaboration for positive behavior support in the home. *Focus on Autism and Other Developmental Disabilities, 17,* 216–228.

O'Neill, R.E., Horner, R.H., Albin, R.W., Sprague, J.R., Storey, K., & Newton, J.S. (1997). *Functional assessment and program development for problem behavior: A practical handbook.* Belmont, CA: Wadsworth.

Paul, A.S. (2002). The importance of understanding the goals of the family. *Journal of Positive Behavior Interventions. 1,* 61–64.

Repp, A.C., & Horner, R.H. (Eds.). (1999). *Functional analysis and problem behavior: From effective assessment to effective support.* Belmont, CA: Wadsworth.

Santarelli, G., Koegel, R.L., Casas, M., & Koegel, L.K. (2001). Culturally diverse families participating in behavior therapy parent education programs for children with developmental disabilities. *Journal of Positive Behavior Interventions, 3,* 120–123.

Scotti, J.R., & Meyer, L.H. (Eds.). (1999). *Behavioral intervention: Principles, models and practices.* Baltimore: Paul H. Brookes Publishing Co.

Sugai, G., & Horner, R. (2002). The evolution of discipline practices: School-wide positive behavior supports. *Child and Family Behavior Therapy, 24,* 23–50.

Sugai, G., Horner, R.H., Dunlap, G., Hieneman, M., Lewis, T.J., Nelson, C.M., et al. (1999). Applying positive behavioral support and functional behavioral assessment in schools. *Journal of Positive Behavior Interventions, 2,* 131–143.

Tobin, T.J. (2005). *Parent's guide to functional assessment* (3rd ed.). Eugene: University of Oregon, College of Education, Educational and Community Supports. Available from the University of Oregon web site, http://darkwing.uoregon.edu/~ttobin

Turnbull, A., Edmonson, H., Griggs, P., Wickham, D., Sailor, W., Freeman, R., et al. (2002). A blueprint for schoolwide positive behavior support: Implementation of three components. *Exceptional Children, 68,* 377–402.

Turnbull, A.P., & Turnbull, R.H., III. (1996). Group action planning as a strategy for providing comprehensive family support. In L.K. Koegel, R.L. Koegel, & G. Dunlap (Eds.), *Positive behavioral support: Including people with difficult behavior in the community* (pp. 99–114). Baltimore: Paul H. Brookes Publishing Co.

Vaughn, B.J., Dunlap, G., Fox, L., Clarke, S., & Bucy, M. (1997). Parent–professional partnership in behavioral support: A case study of community-based interventions. *Journal of The Association for Persons with Severe Handicaps, 22,* 186–197.

Vaughn, B.J., White, R., Johnston, S., & Dunlap, G. (2005). Positive behavior support as a family-centered endeavor. *Journal of Positive Behavior Interventions, 7,* 55–58.

PARENTING RESOURCES

Aron, E.N. (2002). *The highly sensitive child: Helping our children thrive when the world overwhelms them.* New York: Random House.

Baker, B.L., & Brightman, A.J. (2004). *Steps to independence: Teaching everyday skills to children with special needs* (4th ed.). Baltimore: Paul H. Brookes Publishing Co.

Bean, R., & Clemes, H. (1990). *How to teach children responsibility: The whole child series.* Los Angeles: Price Stern Sloan.

Bentzen, W.R. (2005). *Seeing young children: A guide to observing and recording behavior* (5th ed.). Albany, NY: Thomson Delmar Learning.

Brazelton, T.B. (1992). *Touchpoints: Your child's emotional and behavioral development.* Reading, MA: Addison Wesley Higher Educations Group.

Brazelton, T.B., & Sparrow, J. (2003). *Discipline: The Brazelton way, advice from America's favorite pediatrician.* Cambridge, MA: Da Capo Press.

Canter, L. (1995). *What to do when your child won't behave.* Santa Monica, CA: Lee Canter and Associates.

Carter, N., & Kahn, L. (1996). *See how we grow: A report on the status of parent education in the U.S.* Philadelphia: Pew Charitable Trusts.

Clark, L. (1996). *SOS! Help for parents: A practical guide for handling common everyday behavior problems* (2nd ed.). Bowling Green, KY: Parents Press.

Coloroso, B. (2002). *Kids are worth it: Giving your child the gift of inner discipline.* New York: HarperCollins.

Covey, S.R. (1997). *The seven habits of highly effective families.* New York: Golden Books.

Crary, E. (1993). *Without spanking or spoiling: A practical approach to toddler and preschool guidance* (2nd ed.). Seattle: Parenting Press.

Crary, E. (1996). *Help! The kids are at it again: Using kids' quarrels to teach people skills.* Seattle: Parenting Press.

Dietz, M.J., & Whaley, J. (1997). *School, family, and community: Techniques and methods for successful collaboration.* Gaithersburg, MD: Aspen Publishers.

Dinkmeyer, D.C., & McKay, G.D. (1997). *Parent's handbook: Systematic training for effective parenting.* Circle Pines, MN: AGS Publishing.

Divinyi, J.E. (2004). *Discipline that works: Five simple steps.* Peachtree City, GA: The Wellness Connection.

Elias, M.J., Tobias, S.E., & Friedlander, B.S. (2000). *Emotionally intelligent parenting: How to raise a self-disciplined, responsible, socially skilled child.* New York: Three Rivers Press.

Elkind, D. (2001). *The hurried child: Growing up too fast too soon* (3rd ed.). Cambridge, MA: Da Capo Press.

Essa, E. (2003). *A practical guide to solving preschool behavior problems* (5th ed.). Albany, NY: Thomson Delmar Learning.

Faber, A., & Mazlish, E. (1990). *Liberated parents, liberated children: Your guide to a happier family.* New York: HarperCollins.

Faber, A., & Mazlish, E. (1999). *How to talk so kids will listen and listen so kids will talk.* New York: HarperCollins.

Flick, G.L. (2002). *Power parenting for children with ADD/ADHD: A practical parent's guide for managing difficult behaviors.* San Francisco: Jossey-Bass.

Foxman, P. (2004). *The worried child: Recognizing anxiety in children and helping them heal.* Alameda, CA: Hunter House Publishing.

Galinsky, E., & David, J. (1990). *The preschool years: Family strategies that work—from experts and parents.* New York: Random House.

Gordon, T. (2000). *Parent effectiveness training: The proven program for raising responsible children.* New York: Three Rivers Press.

Hyman, I.A. (1997). *The case against spanking: How to discipline your child without hitting.* San Francisco: Jossey-Bass.

Jacobs, D.M., & Jacobs, R. (1999). *Zip your lips. A parents guide to brief and effective communication.* Rockport, MA: Houghton Mifflin.

Kabat-Zinn, M., & Kabat-Zinn, J. (1998). *Everyday blessings: The inner work of mindful parenting.* New York: Hyperion.

Kurcinka, M.S. (1998). *Raising your spirited child: A guide for parents whose child is more intense, sensitive, perceptive, persistent, energetic.* New York: HarperCollins.

Kvols, K.J. (1997). *Redirecting children's behavior* (3rd ed.). Seattle: Parenting Press.

Latham, G.I. (2000). *The power of positive parenting*. Salt Lake City, UT: Northwest Publishing.

Leach, P. (1997). *Your baby and child: From birth to age five*. New York: Alfred A. Knopf.

Maag, J.W. (1996). *Parenting without punishment: Making problem behavior work for you*. Philadelphia: The Charles Press, Publishers.

Maslin, B. (2004). *Picking your battles: Winning strategies for raising well-behaved kids*. New York: St. Martin's Press.

McKay, G.D., & Mabell, S.A. (2004). *Calming the family storm: Anger management for moms, dads, and all the kids*. Atascadero, CA: Impact Publishers.

Nelsen, J., & Delzer, C. (1999). *Positive discipline for single parents: A practical guide to raising children who are responsible, respectful, and resourceful*. New York: Crown Publishing Group.

Nelsen, J., Lott, L., & Glenn, S. (1999). *Positive discipline A–Z: 1001 solutions to everyday parenting problems* (2nd ed.). New York: Three Rivers Press.

Paquette, P.H., & Tuttle, C.G. (1999). *Parenting a child with a behavior problem: A practical and empathetic guide*. Los Angeles: Lowell House.

Popkin, M.H. (1993). *Active parenting today: For parents of 2- to 12-year-olds: Parents' guide*. Kennesaw, GA: Active Parenting Publishers.

Samalin, N., & Whitney, C. (1997). *Loving each one best: A caring and practical approach to raising siblings*. New York: Random House.

Severe, S. (2000). *How to behave so your children will, too!* New York: Penguin Books.

Sgro, V. (2004). *Organize your family's schedule in no time*. Upper Saddle River, NJ: Pearson Education.

Shea, T.M., & Bauer, A.M. (1991). *Parents and teachers of children with exceptionalities: A handbook for collaboration*. Boston: Allyn & Bacon.

Sheridan, S.M. (1998). *Why don't they like me? Helping your child make and keep friends*. Longmont, CO: Sopris West Educational Services.

Shure, M.B. (2001). *Raising a thinking preteen: The "I Can Problem Solve" program for 8- to 12-year-olds*. New York: Henry Holt and Company.

Spencer, P., & Parenting Magazine Editors. (2001). *Parenting: Guide to positive discipline*. New York: Random House.

Stahl, P.M. (2000). *Parenting after divorce: A guide to resolving conflicts and meeting your children's needs*. Atascadero, CA: Impact Publishers.

Thompson, M. (2004). *Mom, they're teasing me: Helping your child solve social problems*. New York: Random House.

Tinglof, C.B. (2002). *The organized parent: 365 simple solutions to managing your home, your time, and your family's life*. Chicago: McGraw-Hill.

Turecki, S. (2000). *The difficult child*. New York: Bantam Dell Publishing Group.

Vernon, A., & Al-Mabuk, R.H. (1995). *What growing up is all about: A parent's guide to child and adolescent development*. Champaign, IL: Research Press.

Weissbluth, M. (2005). *Healthy sleep habits, happy child*. New York: Random House.

Wykoff, J., & Unell, B.C. (2002). *Discipline without shouting or spanking: Practical solutions to the most common preschool behavior problems*. Minnetonka, MN: Meadowbrook Press.

WEB SITES

General

Beach Center on Disability, University of Kansas
http://beachcenter.org

Center for Effective Collaboration and Practice
http://cecp.air.org

Center for Evidence-Based Practice: Young Children with Challenging Behavior
http://challengingbehavior.org

Center on the Social and Emotional Foundations for Early Learning
http://csefel.uiuc.edu

National Dissemination Center for Children with Disabilities
http://www.nichcy.org

Postive Behavior Support Links

Center on Positive Behavioral Interventions and Support
http://www.pbis.org

Journal of Positive Behavior Interventions
http://education.ucsb.edu/autism/jpbi.html

Kansas Institute for Positive Behavior Support
http://www.kipbs.org

Office of Special Education Programs (OSEP) Center on Positive Behavioral Interventions and Supports: Understanding Problem Behavior: An Interactive Tutorial
http://serc.gws.uky.edu/pbis

On-line Academy for Positive Behavioral Support
http://uappbs.apbs.org

Regional Positive Behavior Support Contacts

Stone Soup Group (Alaska)
http://www.stonesoupgroup.org

PBS Project (Florida)
http://flpbs.fmhi.usf.edu

Behavioral Intervention Program (Georgia)
http://www.pbsga.org

LRE for Life (Tennessee)
http://web.utk.edu/~lre4life

Indiana Resource Center for Autism (Indiana)
http://www.iidc.indiana.edu/~irca

Positive Behavior Support Project (Delaware)
http://www.udel.edu/cds/pbs

University of Kentucky and Positive Behavioral Interventions and Supports (Kentucky)
http://www.pbis.org/main.htm

Michigan's Integrated Behavior and Learning Support Initiative (Michigan)
http://cenmi.org/miblsi/Default.asp

Positive Behavior Support in West Virginia (West Virginia)
http://www.as.wvu.edu/wvpbs/

Blank Worksheets of Information-Gathering Tools

Interview Record
Time Chart
Behavior Log
Behavior Support Plan

INTERVIEW RECORD

Talk to the child and/or someone who knows the child well. Ask this person the following questions about the problem behavior, asking additional questions until you fully understand his or her perspective.

What are _____ greatest strengths and interests? (e.g., What does _____ do well, enjoy?)

What specifically is _____ doing that is of concern to you?

Under what circumstances (when, where, with whom) do these behaviors occur most?

Under what circumstances (when, where, with whom) do these behaviors occur least?

What do you think _____ gets or avoids through these behaviors?

Is there anything else you think might be affecting _____ behavior?

☼ TIME CHART

Problem behavior: _____

List the time periods and/or activities in a typical day in the left-hand column and record the dates in the boxes to the right. Mark the block if the behavior occurs during that time period or activity. Use a new column for each recorded day. Record for enough days to notice a pattern in when the behaviors are occurring.

Activity or time of day	Date					

☼ BEHAVIOR LOG

Name: _____ Date: _____

Situation: _____

What happened before	What he or she did	What happened after

BEHAVIOR SUPPORT PLAN for _____

Who will be involved?

Where and when will the plan be used?

Goals

What exactly our child says or does that is a problem:	How often and/or how long these behaviors occur:

Broad goals for our child and our family:

Summary Statements

When this occurs:	Our child does:	To get/avoid:

(continued on next page)

Parenting with Positive Behavior Support
A Practical Guide to Resolving Your Child's Difficult Behavior
by Meme Hieneman, Karen Childs, and Jane Sergay.

(continued from previous page)

 BEHAVIOR SUPPORT PLAN for _____

Strategies (based on summary statements)

Prevent problems: (What changes will we make in order to avoid problems, make difficult situations better, or prompt appropriate behavior?)	**Replace behavior:** (What skills will we teach in order to replace the problem behavior?)	**Manage consequences:** (What responses will we use in order to reward positive behavior and not problem behavior?)

Is a plan needed to ensure the safety of our child, other people, and the surroundings? _____ yes _____ no   If so, describe strategies:

Other support needed to improve our child's life:

(continued from previous page)

☀ BEHAVIOR SUPPORT PLAN for _____

Action Plan

What needs to be done?	By whom?	By when?

How will the plan be monitored?

Parenting with Positive Behavior Support
A Practical Guide to Resolving Your Child's Difficult Behavior
by Meme Hieneman, Karen Childs, and Jane Sergay.

Behavior Support Plans for the Case Studies

Behavior Support Plan for Deon
Behavior Support Plan for James
Behavior Support Plan for Brittany
Behavior Support Plan for Zoë
Behavior Support Plan for Isobel
Behavior Support Plan for Michael

BEHAVIOR SUPPORT PLAN for	Deon

Who will be involved?

Adrienne, Darell, Deon's older brothers, and the other adults who care for him (baby sitter, extended family)

Where and when will the plan be used?

When the person caring for Deon (usually Adrienne) needs to focus his or her attention on something or someone else, within the home but also in the community

Goals

What exactly our child says or does that is a problem:	How often and/or how long these behaviors occur:
Whining: using high-pitched "eh" sounds or repetitive words (e.g., saying "up, up") Clinging: grabbing around legs, pulling on clothing	On the average, four times per day and for long periods (almost half the time Adrienne spends preparing dinner)

Broad goals for our child and our family:

Deon will play by himself for 10 minutes (e.g., while Adrienne cooks dinner). Adrienne will be able to do some of the activities she has been missing on a daily basis (e.g., have conversations with friends, take a shower).

Summary Statements

When this occurs:	Our child does:	To get/avoid:
When Adrienne tries to do something other than interact with Deon (e.g., talk on telephone, cook dinner).	Whines, clings to her legs, and repeatedly asks to be picked up.	His whining gets her attention (she stops doing other things and talks to or soothes him).

These behaviors are especially likely during time periods when things are chaotic, there are unfamiliar people in the area, or Deon is hungry, tired or sick.

(continued on next page)

(continued from previous page)

BEHAVIOR SUPPORT PLAN for   _Deon_

Strategies (based on summary statements)

Prevent problems:	Replace behavior:	Manage consequences:
(What changes will we make in order to avoid problems, make difficult situations better, or prompt appropriate behavior?)	(What skills will we teach in order to replace the problem behavior?)	(What responses will we use in order to reward positive behavior and not problem behavior?)
Provide Deon with comfort or help before beginning an activity that requires undivided attention.	*Encourage Deon to use his words (e.g., "Ma, help") or point to a desired object when he wants something.*	*Only respond to Deon's demands for attention when he uses his words or gestures.*
Tell Deon what behavior is expected of him during that time.	*Teach Deon to play by himself for brief time periods (e.g., show him how to use his toys and then have him practice using toys or looking at books by himself).*	*Ignore Deon while he is whining (send him to another room if necessary) and respond only when he stops whining.*
Give Deon special activities or toys to use that can keep his attention during this time.		*When Deon is playing quietly by himself, make a point of praising him and giving him a little attention (e.g., "It looks like you are having fun with your toys!").*

Is a plan needed to ensure the safety of our child, other people, and the surroundings? _____ yes   _✓_ no   If so, describe strategies:

Other support needed to improve our child's life:

Make sure Deon gets naps, meals and snacks, and medical treatment when he needs them. Plan one-to-one time with him throughout the day (e.g. stop, get down on the floor with him, and share toys, snuggle, or talk to him about what he is doing for a few minutes).

(continued on next page)

(continued from previous page)

BEHAVIOR SUPPORT PLAN for   Deon

Action Plan

What needs to be done?	By whom?	By when?
Put together a special box of toys for Deon to play with when Adrienne or another caregiver is doing other things.	Adrienne	In 1 week
Talk to Deon about what activities will be going on around him and what behavior he is to use (remind him to use his words when he needs help).	Adrienne	Daily as needed
Teach Deon to play by himself (demonstrate with toys and books).	Adrienne	In 1 week

How will the plan be monitored?

Adrienne will keep a daily journal reflecting on when, where, and with whom Deon's whining occurs and will review the results with Darell every evening after Deon is asleep.

BEHAVIOR SUPPORT PLAN for	James

Who will be involved?

Lauren, Rick, Julie, James's peers, and the other adults who interact with James (the parents of James's peers and James's karate instructor, Mr. Kent)

Where and when will the plan be used?

During afternoons, evenings, and weekends where James is at home, at sports events, and in the neighborhood

Goals

What exactly our child says or does that is a problem:	How often and/or how long these behaviors occur:
Yelling: speaking with a raised voice	On the average, James's yelling and teasing happen five to six times per day; aggressing happens approximately two times each day.
Teasing: calling names, making threats, taking items from his peers or holding items out of their reach	
Hurting others: hitting and kicking both people and objects; throwing objects; choking people	

Broad goals for our child and our family:

James will be able to play unsupervised with Julie and with his peers.

James's relationships with Julie and his peers will improve (e.g., other children will be willing to visit James at home).

James will continue to be involved in karate practice and other sports.

Summary Statements

When this occurs:	Our child does:	To get/avoid:
When James interacts with younger peers in less structured situations for more than 10 minutes.	Yells, refuses to share toys and activities with other people, calls others names, and teases others; if his peers try to defend themselves, James hits, kicks, or chokes them or throws things at them.	To get others to react to him (e.g., cry, run away), which he seems to enjoy.

(continued on next page)

(continued from previous page)

BEHAVIOR SUPPORT PLAN for James

Strategies (based on summary statements)

Prevent problems:	**Replace behavior:**	**Manage consequences:**
(What changes will we make in order to avoid problems, make difficult situations better, or prompt appropriate behavior?)	(What skills will we teach in order to replace the problem behavior?)	(What responses will we use in order to reward positive behavior and not problem behavior?)
Monitor James with other children more closely and intervene before he hurts them.	*Teach James appropriate ways to get emotional reactions from other children (e.g., telling jokes).*	*Encourage Julie and James's peers to walk away from James or go get an adult when James starts teasing or yelling at them.*
Establish rules for playing together and review them with all the children and the adults who may be supervising them.	*Teach James how to play appropriately with other children, share his belongings, and resolve his problems with words (e.g., "Can you try to do it this way?").*	*Reward James (and Julie) for playing together nicely by letting them do an activity they particularly enjoy.*
Interrupt play after about 10 minutes and have the children change activities to discourage problems before they begin.	*Teach James to relax (e.g., concentrate on breathing deeply) and walk away from the problem when angry.*	*Continue to use time-outs when James hurts his peers but stop spanking him.*
Encourage the smaller children to walk away from James rather than fight back.	*Coach James to use these skills with Julie (e.g., as they go off to play, ask James to explain how he will handle disagreements in advance).*	*Monitor James's playing with other children and reward him for handling problems well (e.g. with praise, extra play time).*

Is a plan needed to ensure the safety of our child, other people, and the surroundings? __✓__ yes ____ no   If so, describe strategies:

Intervene quickly when James begins to hurt others (e.g., choking, kicking, hitting people and objects; throwing things toward Julie or other children). This might mean using words to direct him or even physically taking him to his room until he calms down.

Other support needed to improve our child's life:

Try to find activities that are of common interest to James, Julie, and James's peers; do those activities with them in an attempt to improve their relationships (e.g., marking off a foursquare court in the driveway, set up a roller-hockey goal and game at the end of the street).

(continued on next page)

(continued from previous page)

BEHAVIOR SUPPORT PLAN for   <u>James</u>

Action Plan

What needs to be done?	By whom?	By when?
Establish rules for playing together.	Lauren, Rick, Mr. Kent, James, and Julie	This weekend
Review rules for playing together.	Lauren, Rick, and Mr. Kent	Before each play time
Talk to the other children about walking away from James instead of fighting.	Lauren, Rick, Mr. Kent, and the parents of James's peers	Before the next time the children play
Interrupt play after 10 minutes and change the activity.	Lauren, Rick, Mr. Kent, and the parents of James's peers	When playing

How will the plan be monitored?

The adult observing the activity will rate how well James plays with other children each day (3 = great, 2 = okay, 1 = lousy). This rating will be reviewed with James every weekend.

BEHAVIOR SUPPORT PLAN for   Brittany

Who will be involved?

Nathan, Margaret, and the other adults who interact with Brittany (the recreation program supervisor and staff, Brittany's general education and special education teachers)

Where and when will the plan be used?

During activities at home, the recreation center, and school

Goals

What exactly our child says or does that is a problem:	How often and/or how long these behaviors occur:
Refusing: not participating in activities, especially in conversations and interactions, physical activities, and household chores Talking obsessively: focusing most of her conversations on the topic of outer space	On a typical day, Brittany participates in one of five nonacademic activities at school, two of five activities at the recreation center, and approximately half of required activities at home. She interacts with an average of two people per day, with the topic of the conversation almost always outer space.

Broad goals for our child and our family:

Each night, Brittany will eat dinner with Nathan and Margaret and do a few basic chores around the house.

Brittany will participate in activities at the recreation center four out of five days and will become involved in other community activities.

Brittany will have conversations about topics other than outer space every day.

Summary Statements

When this occurs:	Our child does:	To get/avoid:
When Brittany is asked to participate in physical activities, do chores around the house, or talk with others on topics other than outer space.	Ignores the request, talks about outer space, or (if pressured) cries or hums loudly.	Brittany's behavior tends to successfully help her get out of participating in certain activities (e.g., chores, unfamiliar activities) or social interactions (e.g., talking about topics she does not enjoy).

Brittany is more resistant to participating in activities when she has to stop doing an activity she likes, the situation is demanding, or the expectations are not clear.

(continued on next page)

(continued from previous page)

BEHAVIOR SUPPORT PLAN for   Brittany

Strategies (based on summary statements)

Prevent problems:

(What changes will we make in order to avoid problems, make difficult situations better, or prompt appropriate behavior?)

Work with Brittany to develop a schedule of chores and activities so she can see what she needs to do daily.

Give Brittany a clear warning or conversation guide before asking her to stop reading about or discussing outer space (e.g., "We are going to talk about another topic now.").

Have Brittany keep her books and personal digital assistant (PDA) out of sight when doing other activities.

Describe social situations/ expectations clearly before Brittany takes part in them; rehearse different ways in which she can participate.

Ask Brittany's peers to explain situations to her when she seems uncomfortable.

Replace behavior:

(What skills will we teach in order to replace the problem behavior?)

Encourage Brittany to write down and follow her daily schedule, record activities and topics of conversations, and rate how she did in the different situations.

Teach Brittany to vocalize appropriate requests and queries (e.g., "I need a little time." "This is hard for me.") when she is uncomfortable with a situation and needs a break or to ask for clarification regarding expectations.

Teach Brittany social skills for talking with friends (e.g., how to start and stop a conversation).

Manage consequences:

(What responses will we use in order to reward positive behavior and not problem behavior?)

Allow Brittany to have private time to read or use the computer as a reward after completing required chores and activities or when she asks to be excused appropriately.

Allow Brittany to discuss a topic of her interest after she engages in a conversation on a different topic.

Avoid stopping interactions or withdrawing demands when Brittany engages in inappropriate behavior.

Have Brittany record her interactions with peers and adults (e.g., who she talked to, what they said).

Allow Brittany a special treat or reward (e.g., to go to the library or earn credit toward the purchase of a new book) when she joins in on all of her activities and interacts well with people during a set time period.

Is a plan needed to ensure the safety of our child, other people, and the surroundings? ____ yes _√_ no If so, describe strategies:

(continued on next page)

(continued from previous page)

BEHAVIOR SUPPORT PLAN for <u>Brittany</u>

Other support needed to improve our child's life:

Review Brittany's daily schedule to make sure that she has plenty of time to do the activities she enjoys (e.g., reading, playing on the computer) at home, school, and the recreation center. Work with her to expand her interests to other topics (maybe initially related to outer space). Look for a science club in which she can interact with peers who are interested in similar topics.

Action Plan		
What needs to be done?	By whom?	By when?
Develop schedule of chores and activities and allow Brittany to select her chores and activities among options.	Brittany, Nathan, and Margaret (with input from other adults)	Every Sunday
Set up Brittany's PDA for recording a daily schedule and teach her how to use the schedule.	Brittany and Nathan	Next Saturday
Develop a list of appropriate topics of conversation and practice talking about those topics with Brittany.	Brittany, Nathan, Margaret, and Brittany's special education teacher	Within 2 weeks
Allow Brittany to earn credit toward purchasing new books and set up a chart that allows her to monitor her earnings.	Brittany and Nathan	After meeting all goals for 1 week
Review strategies for preventing problems and responding appropriately to behaviors.	Everyone	Every 2 weeks
Explain to Brittany social situations and skills for having a conversation (including how she can end one when uncomfortable).	Nathan, Margaret, and Brittany's teachers	Within 2 weeks, with regular reminders

How will the plan be monitored?

Brittany will use self-monitoring. She will record the following in her PDA: what interactions she has, with whom she interacts, and which topics of conversation were followed. Every Sunday, Brittany and Nathan will review the previous week and record the coming week's schedule of activities.

BEHAVIOR SUPPORT PLAN for   _Zoë_

Who will be involved?

Helena, Alex, and Zoë's baby sitters as necessary

Where and when will the plan be used?

At home during bedtime

Goals

What exactly our child says or does that is a problem:	How often and/or how long these behaviors occur:
Wandering: leaving her bedroom in the middle of the night	At least an hour almost every night
Disrupting: whining, calling out for Helena or Alex, and not going to sleep at bedtime	

Broad goals for our child and our family:

Zoë will fall asleep independently and remain in her own bedroom through the entire night.

Bedtime will be a happy, peaceful period for the whole family.

The family will be rested, relaxed, and generally comfortable with each other.

Summary Statements

When this occurs:	Our child does:	To get/avoid:
When Helena or Alex put Zoë to bed in her own bedroom to go to sleep by herself.	Cries, whines, gets out of bed, and becomes destructive and disruptive.	She works to get Helena or Alex to stay in her bedroom with her and avoid going to sleep by herself.

This behavior is especially likely to occur when the rest of Zoë's family stays awake after she is put to bed and when she can overhear Helena and Alex playing with baby Kora.

(continued on next page)

(continued from previous page)

BEHAVIOR SUPPORT PLAN for   *Zoë*

Strategies (based on summary statements)

Prevent problems:	Replace behavior:	Manage consequences:
(What changes will we make in order to avoid problems, make difficult situations better, or prompt appropriate behavior?)	(What skills will we teach in order to replace the problem behavior?)	(What responses will we use in order to reward positive behavior and not problem behavior?)
Spend more quality time with Zoë earlier in the evening, before bedtime.	Encourage Zoë to stay in bed after Helena and Alex have left the room and remain quiet until she falls asleep.	Come check on Zoë after 10 minutes and give her snuggles (that time will be extended gradually until Zoë no longer needs them to come check on her at all).
Change bath time so that it is not immediately before bedtime.	Teach Zoë to calm and to comfort herself if she wakes in the night by playing music, looking at books, looking at the picture by her bed, singing quietly to herself, playing mental games, and so forth.	Let Zoë choose a special activity to do with Helena when Kora is napping the next day, but only if she stays in her bedroom all night.
Make the house quiet when Zoë is going to sleep.		Allow Zoë to put a sticker on her refrigerator chart when she used positive behavior the night before.
Allow Zoë to listen to soft music when she is going to sleep.		Let Zoë pick a special outing with Helena and Alex after she has used positive behavior for a whole week.
Allow Zoë to pick a picture to put beside her bed to look at when going to sleep.		Respond to her behavior by: The first time Zoë leaves her bedroom, remind her how she must earn her treat and walk her back to her bed with minimal interaction and attention; the second time Zoë leaves her bedroom, walk her back to bed and close her bedroom door (remind her that the door will be opened later that night
Delay Zoë's bedtime so that Alex can be home to help watch Kora while Helena puts Zoë to bed or put Zoë to bed while Helena watches Kora.		
Allow Zoë to pick a stuffed animal (a bedtime buddy) to keep her company while she is sleeping.		
Work to establish a clear and consistent night routine.		

(continued on next page)

(continued from previous page)

BEHAVIOR SUPPORT PLAN for   *Zoë*

Strategies (based on summary statements) (continued)

Prevent problems:	Replace behavior:	Manage consequences:
(What changes will we make in order to avoid problems, make difficult situations better, or prompt appropriate behavior?)	(What skills will we teach in order to replace the problem behavior?)	(What responses will we use in order to reward positive behavior and not problem behavior?)
		if she stays quietly in bed).
		Ignore Zoë if she cries or yells.
		Stop Zoë immediately if she does something dangerous, remove the broken items from her bedroom, and quickly leave her alone in her bedroom.

Is a plan needed to ensure the safety of our child, other people, and the surroundings? __√__ yes _____ no   If so, describe strategies:

If Zoë's behavior becomes dangerous (throwing things, jumping on and off the bed) remain calm, stop her by removing the items she is throwing, and exit the room quickly with minimal interaction and attention.

Other support needed to improve our child's life:

Enroll Zoë in a "Mommy and Me" class at the local YMCA as an activity in which only she (and not Kora) can participate.

(continued on next page)

(continued from previous page)

BEHAVIOR SUPPORT PLAN for	Zoë	
Action Plan		
What needs to be done?	By whom?	By when?
Purchase a tape player and obtain relaxation tapes and manuals on relaxation from the library.	Alex	The next day during his lunch hour
Tell Zoë about the new bedtime routine.	Helena and Alex	The next day
Practice the new bedtime routine and use the relaxation techniques.	Helena, Alex, and Zoë	During Kora's naptime
Create a chart so that Zoë can track her own behavior and put it on the refrigerator.	Zoë and Helena	The next day
Select picture for Zoë to put beside her bed.	Zoë and Helena	In 2 days
Review the plan and make a schedule for checking on the progress.	Helena and Alex	In 2 days

How will the plan be monitored?

Helena and Alex will spend a few minutes each morning discussing what behaviors occurred the night before, reviewing the behavior chart, and considering how well everyone carried out the plan. If after 1 week Zoë's behavior has shown improvement, they will discuss the progress weekly instead of daily.

BEHAVIOR SUPPORT PLAN for _Isobel_

Who will be involved?

Simone, Luis, Aarón, and Maria

Where and when will the plan be used?

Primarily at home and throughout the day, although monitoring will also be done as needed at school and in the community

Goals

What exactly our child says or does that is a problem:	How often and/or how long these behaviors occur:
Defying: ignoring instructions and breaking rules Disrespecting: talking rudely to, arguing with, and using sarcasm on her parents	Both behaviors occur at least three times each day and more frequently on the weekend

Broad goals for our child and our family:

Isobel will follow the house rules, accept the limits Simone and Luis impose, contribute to the household, and interact positively with her family members.

The home environment will be peaceful and harmonious most of the time.

Isobel will become involved in positive school and community activities.

Isobel will gain more freedom and independence.

Summary Statements

When this occurs:	Our child does:	To get/avoid:
When Simone or Luis ask Isobel to do an activity she does not like or question her about her activities.	Ignores and/or talks (or screams) rudely at them.	To avoid doing the activities and having interactions she does not enjoy and to gain control over the circumstances around her.

Simone and Luis recognize that Isobel's pattern of behavior might have been made worse by their inconsistent expectations and lack of supervision.

(continued on next page)

(continued from previous page)

BEHAVIOR SUPPORT PLAN for   Isobel

Strategies (based on summary statements)

Prevent problems:	Replace behavior:	Manage consequences:
(What changes will we make in order to avoid problems, make difficult situations better, or prompt appropriate behavior?)	(What skills will we teach in order to replace the problem behavior?)	(What responses will we use in order to reward positive behavior and not problem behavior?)

Prevent problems:

Review the current responsibilities expected of Isobel and establish a clear list of what is required of her around the house and in the community.

Clarify which of the activities Isobel is able to do are privileges and which are rights.

Meet as a family to establish a family vision and expectations that every family member must meet. Write the vision and expectations down and post them in a public place.

Set up a dry erase board for family members to communicate their activities and where-abouts (where they are going, what they are doing, who they are with, and when they will return).

Replace behavior:

Teach Isobel that independence requires responsibility by linking meeting expectations to greater freedoms and opportunities.

Teach Isobel to talk calmly when expressing concerns (e.g., identifying an appropriate time to talk, using a calm voice to tell her parents she wants to talk about a concern).

Model the kind of interactions desired from Isobel (e.g., use calm, quiet voices).

Manage consequences:

Allow Isobel to do a special activity from a generated list each week that she meets the expectations.

Allow Isobel access to privileges if and only if she: cleans up after herself, speaks respectfully to her family members, adheres to curfew, joins the family for dinner at least three days per week, completes her household chores, and records her whereabouts on the dry erase board.

Is a plan needed to ensure the safety of our child, other people, and the surroundings? _____ yes   √ no   If so, describe strategies:

(continued on next page)

(continued from previous page)

BEHAVIOR SUPPORT PLAN for   Isobel

Other support needed to improve our child's life:

Explore the possibilities of Isobel auditioning for a part in a community theater production, obtaining a part-time job, or finding other constructive after-school activities to provide her with greater autonomy and responsibility.

	Action Plan	
What needs to be done?	By whom?	By when?
Develop a written contract specifying Isobel's expectations, privileges, and consequences for inappropriate behavior.	Simone, Luis, and Isobel	This weekend
Block out time on Saturdays to provide transportation for Isobel's special activities.	Simone	Immediately
Hold family meetings.	All the family	On weekends
Meet with Isobel to establish more opportunities for her independence.	Simone, Luis, and Isobel	After Isobel's behavior has improved for a few weeks

How will the plan be monitored?

Simone and Luis will discuss how the plan is working and will talk periodically with Isobel's teachers and peers in order to consider how Isobel has been interacting with others, meeting expectations, communicating her whereabouts, and voicing concerns appropriately. Each week, they will ask Isobel how she has been doing and expand her opportunities for freedom and independence based on her meeting the expectations. They will also review their own consistency in their expectations and how they use the plan. During family meetings, they will discuss the overall atmosphere of the home and acknowledge any positive changes.

BEHAVIOR SUPPORT PLAN for ___Michael___

Who will be involved?

Deborah, the carpool parents and their children, and Michael's teachers: Ms. Miller and Mrs. Sharp

Where and when will the plan be used?

At home, at school, and when using the carpool; especially during morning transitions

Goals

What exactly our child says or does that is a problem:	How often and/or how long these behaviors occur:
Procrastinating: staying in his bed so that he is not ready for school in time	Misses carpool due to being late two or three times per week; whines and ignores daily
Ignoring: failing to respond to specific requests to get ready for school	
Whining: complaining and begging his mother for special favors in the morning	

Broad goals for our child and our family:

Michael will develop independence and personal responsibility for getting himself ready for school in the morning.

Michael and Deborah will arrive on time for school, work, and other engagements on a consistent basis and will have more peace and less conflict in their relationship, especially in the morning.

Deborah will spend more time attending to her own personal needs, including leaving the house in the evenings to spend time with her friends.

Summary Statements

When this occurs:	Our child does:	To get/avoid:
When Deborah gives Michael instructions about getting ready for school.	Ignores, stays in bed, and whines.	To get increasingly more attention from Deborah and to put off having to go to school.

Michael's behavior while getting ready for the day seems to relate to his social and academic difficulties at school.

(continued on next page)

(continued from previous page)

BEHAVIOR SUPPORT PLAN for   Michael

Strategies (based on summary statements)

Prevent problems:	Replace behavior:	Manage consequences:
(What changes will we make in order to avoid problems, make difficult situations better, or prompt appropriate behavior?)	(What skills will we teach in order to replace the problem behavior?)	(What responses will we use in order to reward positive behavior and not problem behavior?)

Prevent problems:

Schedule more personalized time with Michael at times other than when he is getting ready for school.

Have Michael shower at night rather than in the morning in order to save time.

Create a clear morning routine and morning expectations.

Remind Michael about the rewards he can get if he uses more positive behavior.

Replace behavior:

Teach Michael to get up from bed and ready for school with limited direction.

Encourage Michael to ask for and plan time with Deborah appropriately (e.g., "I know we are in a hurry now, but could we watch a movie together later tonight?").

Develop Michael's skills for initiating tasks, following through with his responsibilities, and interacting with other children.

Manage consequences:

Praise Michael when he gets ready independently; limit attention when he is ignoring his responsibilities.

Give Michael a hot breakfast and do a 10-minute activity with him if he is ready for school on time.

Let Michael choose an activity that he can do with Deborah on the weekend and drive him to school as an extra treat next week if he is consistently ready and on time for school for a week.

Ask the children and parents in the carpool group to greet Michael warmly when he arrives on time.

Ask Ms. Miller to give Michael a homework pass that will excuse Michael from doing one homework assignment if he arrives to class on time and completes all his work at school for a set time period.

Is a plan needed to ensure the safety of our child, other people, and the surroundings? _____ yes   _√_ no   If so, describe strategies:

(continued on next page)

(continued from previous page)

BEHAVIOR SUPPORT PLAN for ___Michael___

Other support needed to improve our child's life:

Together, Michael and Deborah will attend at least two social activities with other people each month in an effort to develop more friendships in their lives. Other ways to improve Michael's life include determining if he can be supported in his general education language arts class, rather than depend on his special education class; developing goals and plans to encourage him to find friendships with his peers (e.g., play dates with carpool kids); and helping him complete his schoolwork more quickly.

	Action Plan	
What needs to be done?	By whom?	By when?
Talk to Michael about the plan, making sure to discuss possible activities that they can do together.	Deborah and Michael	By Saturday
Talk with Ms. Miller and Mrs. Sharp about Michael's academic needs and ways he can develop friendships.	Deborah, Ms. Miller, and Mrs. Sharp	By Monday
Talk with the other parents in the carpool about the new plan, give each parent a small container of Legos for Michael to play with when the carpool picks him up.	Deborah and the other carpool parents	By Sunday
Share the strategies developed with the aid of Ms. Miller and Mrs. Sharp with Michael's Sunday School teacher.	Deborah	Sunday after church
Remind Michael of the morning expectations.	Deborah	Before going to bed and again when Michael wakes up

How will the plan be monitored?

Deborah will make notes on her calendar at work about how the mornings went that day and will mark the dates when Michael plays with a friend. She will communicate weekly with his school about his progress, and she will check with carpool parents on their observations about Michael occasionally. Every week, Michael and Deborah will also discuss the events and situations going on at home and school.

APPENDIX C

Examples of Problem Solving for Difficult Family Routines

Mealtimes
Greeting Others
Playing Independently

Problem-Solving Situations and Routines: Mealtimes

What are the goals for our family (e.g., the changes desired, the behaviors of concern) during this difficult period?

> To eat peacefully as a family, with everyone remaining at the table, eating his or her food, and engaging in pleasant conversation.

What patterns might be contributing to our behavior as a family during this routine? The circumstances associated with our best and worst times:

> Best: The children are hungry, everyone understands the expectations, and everyone likes the meal.
> Worst: The children are full, tired, sick, or dislike the meal; the parents are focused on their own conversation.

The outcomes causing patterns to continue:

> The parents allow everyone to eat his or her preferred foods (e.g., snacks, desserts) regardless of whether everyone has finished the meal.
> The children get attention from the parents for misbehaving at the table.

Given our understanding about the patterns surrounding problem routines, what strategies might we put in place to

Prevent problems?

> Encourage the children to use the bathroom and take care of other business that might interfere with the dinner prior to coming to the table.
> Remind the children of the mealtime expectations when they sit down.
> Prepare meals that the children will eat; provide different food options if meal is new or unusual.
> Give the children reasonable portions of food (e.g., use small plates).
> Limit the children's snacking between meals (e.g., no food before breakfast, after 10:30 A.M., or after 4:30 P.M.). Limit the consumption of sweets at other times.

Replace behavior?

> Remind the children to remain seated during the entire meal.
> Encourage the children to eat meals without complaining about what meal was served or to request something else where appropriate.
> Participate in family conversation about daily events.

Manage consequences?

> If the children remain at the table and finish everything on their plates by the time the kitchen has been tidied after the meal, they may have a dessert.
> Praise the children frequently for using positive behavior, and provide feedback to them for eating and sitting nicely.
> Focus the conversation on the children when they are behaving appropriately.
> If the children play with their food, fail to use their utensils properly, or become disruptive (e.g., argue), give them one warning and then ask them to leave the table.
> If they leave the table, they may not have dessert and must finish their meal after everyone else has left the table.

Problem-Solving Situations and Routines: Greeting Others

What are the goals for our family (e.g., the changes desired, the behaviors of concern) during this difficult period?

For everyone in the family to greet other people warmly, respond appropriately during conversations, and use proper manners (e.g., say "please" and "thank you").

What patterns might be contributing to our behavior as a family during this routine?
The circumstances associated with our best and worst times:

Best: The children understand the expectations and routines; the people they interact with are familiar.

Worst: The children are addressed by strangers; the parents fail to model appropriate greeting behaviors.

The outcomes causing patterns to continue:

The children avoid having to interact with people and responding to questions.

Given our understanding about the patterns surrounding problem routines, what strategies might we put in place to
Prevent problems?

Model positive greetings with friends and family members every time (e.g., when a neighbor comes over for a chat, when the children wake up in the morning, when out in public places, when extended family members visit).

Prepare for social situations by discussing who will be there and what behavior is expected (role play if necessary).

Minimize distractions when greeting others (e.g., make sure the television, the radio, or a video game is not on).

Clarify that the children may greet strangers only when the parents are present.

Replace behavior?

Respond to greetings by saying hello and, when appropriate, shaking hands.

Say the word "please" when asking for something and the phrase "thank you" when receiving something.

Answer questions clearly; say "I do not know" if the question cannot be answered.

Make eye contact when speaking with another person.

Manage consequences?

Quietly praise the children for greeting, responding, and using good manners with other people.

Do not let the children avoid interacting with other people by answering for them if they seem unwilling or slow to respond—require the children to respond to questions and use manners even if the behavior is delayed.

Problem-Solving Situations and Routines: Playing Independently

What are the goals for our family (e.g., the changes desired, the behaviors of concern) during this difficult period?

>   For the children to play alone and with other children for reasonable periods of time (e.g., 45 minutes) without behavior problems (e.g., arguing, breaking house rules).

What patterns might be contributing to our behavior as a family during the routine? The circumstances associated with our best and worst times:

>   Best: The children are with particular friends, they are doing activities they enjoy, and their play has clear limits.

>   Worst: The children are playing with friends who have behavior problems and play-time is unstructured.

The outcomes causing patterns to continue:

>   The children obtain attention from adults and/or get access to the item or activity they were arguing about.

Given our understanding about the patterns surrounding problem routines, what strategies might we put in place to

Prevent problems?

>   Let the children know when their parents will be unavailable and for how long.

>   Suggest activities the children may do while their parents are otherwise engaged.

>   Remind the children of the rules about fighting and the problem-solving steps for conflicts.

>   If the playtime is near snack time, set the snack out or let the children know what snack they are allowed to have.

>   Explain any limits to play (e.g., no watching television, stay inside the house, the kitchen-area is off limits).

>   Provide parameters for when the children should get an adult (e.g., if one child has asked another child to stop doing an action and that child continues, if the children cannot resolve a conflict with words, if a child has gotten hurt).

>   Check on the children periodically (e.g., every 15–20 minutes, more often with new or unfamiliar friends).

>   Limit total playtime to a reasonable period (e.g., 2 hours).

Replace behavior?

>   Play independently with toys, games, and each other.

>   Resolve conflicts calmly and fairly and without aggression.

>   Follow the household rules and limits set by the parents or other adults.

>   Get help from an adult when needed—for example, when unsure if a particular play is acceptable, new play ideas are needed, help is needed to resolve a conflict, someone gets hurt, or uncomfortable about the play.

Manage consequences?

>   Praise and encourage creativity and independence in play when checking on the children; if the children would welcome it, play with them briefly.

>   Spend concentrated time with the children after independent playtime.

>   Talk with the children after the play dates so that they can discuss how the time went and work through any concerns.

>   Separate the children if they fight or break the rules.

Index

Page numbers followed by *a, f,* and *t* indicate information presented in activities, figures, and tables, respectively.